no woman is allergic to

Diamonds

and other cynicisms

I0416082

by MACABEE DEAN

HaSakin Press
Ramat Gan, Israel

Published by HaSakin Press in cooperation with Trafford Publishing.

Note: If any reader would like to comment, send a letter to me at Box 7689, Ramat Gan, 52175, Israel. I do not open emails from unknown sources.There are too many virus-dedicated distorted brains in the world.

National Library of Canada Cataloguing in Publication Data

Dean, Macabee
        No woman is allergic to diamonds / written by Macabee
Dean.
        ISBN 1-4120-0184-6
        1. Aphorisms and apothegms. I. Title.
PN6271.D42 2003   082   C2003-
901848-2

TRAFFORD

This book was published *on-demand* in cooperation with Trafford Publishing.
On-demand publishing is a unique process and service of making a book available for retail sale to the public taking advantage of on-demand manufacturing and Internet marketing. **On-demand publishing** includes promotions, retail sales, manufacturing, order fulfilment, accounting and collecting royalties on behalf of the author.

Suite 6E, 2333 Government St., Victoria, B.C. V8T 4P4, CANADA
Phone   250-383-6864   Toll-free   1-888-232-4444 (Canada & US)
Fax   250-383-6804   E-mail   sales@trafford.com
Web site   www.trafford.com   TRAFFORD PUBLISHING IS A DIVISION OF TRAFFORD
HOLDINGS LTD.
Trafford Catalogue #03-0552   www.trafford.com/robots/03-0552.html

10   9   8   7   6   5   4   3

Dedicated to a Grand Master of the Art

Georg Christoph Lichtenberg (1742–1799), German physicist and author who wrote:
"There can hardly be a stranger commodity in the world than books. Printed by people who don't understand them; sold by people who don't understand them; bound, criticized and read by people who don't understand them; and now even written by people who don't understand them."

also dedicated to Andrew Jackson and to H.W. Fowler

Andrew Jackson, the Seventh President of the United States, said:
"It's a damned poor mind that can think of only one way to spell a word."

H.W. Fowler, acknowledged master of the English language, wrote:
"It is the second-rate writers, whose intent rather on expressing themselves prettily than on conveying their meaning clearly… that are chiefly open to the allurement of elegant variation."

And as for the Teachers of the English Language who for generations have inflicted a "cruel and unusual" punishment on their students by forcing them to learn the stupidities of English spelling—well, may they all suffer from insufferable spouses.

Table of Contents

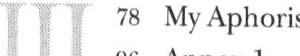

Foreword

This mini-primer is dedicated to those who already write (or utter) short, stinging, penetrating comments, or would like to adopt this pastime.

The suggestions are divided into two main parts.

The first part is aimed at those persons who already compose aphorisms, either steadily or erratically, who find their spring is running dry.

The second part is for those wishing to embark on this hobby and need semi-mechanical means to get them started.

Steady producers should read the second part to get a glimpse of how their minds "may" work—when it works.

One word of advice. Always read with a sharpened pencil in your hand. Make notes in the numerous blank spaces provided: at the end of chapters, in the blank spaces between many paragraphs, in the margins, between lines, and let the notes be both constructive and destructive. When you finish with this lightweight tome, each page should be an unholy mess. Even doodle, if this helps you to concentrate.

One request from the reader. If you lose interest, if you find this booklet boring, don't toss it into the nearest waste basket; give it to an intelligent friend. We are sure you have several, either real or pseudo. But if you decide to continue, take things easy. Unless, of course, reining in to half pace your normal energy output will give you an ulcer or a heart attack. If you motor says gallop, then gallop; if your motor says crawl, then crawl.

Pace yourself to your own internal engine.
You know yourself best.

Or if you don't yet know your own personality, ask your spouse after a bitter spat in which you've stupidly unleashed an accumulation of petty annoyances. Your spouse will certainly describe a personality you've never met, and perhaps never want to meet, at least socially.

Let's say that the worse comes to the worse, and you realize that your aphorisms are frail. Well, you are in the same boat as countless persons who get tremendous satisfaction from painting so-called masterpieces no one wants to look at, no one cares to read, and making speeches no one listens to.

Self-fulfillment is its own reward. It also builds character. (Come on now, let's come clean. Have you ever stopped to think what you will do with all that "character"?)

And let's not forget that if your aphorisms are good or bad, expressing your thoughts in a solid form might not change the world, but it will certainly help you pinpoint your frustrations so you can better understand yourself, and the world.

You can always bask in your hard earned wisdoms and tell yourself that future generations will discover them and raise a statue to honor you, while tearing your generation to pieces for failing to realize your genius.

And if you succeed, as we are sure you will, there is nothing like a well-polished aphorism that cuts like a diamond to bestow on you a feeling of joy each time you reread it. You can even fool yourself into believing that you have left indelible footprints on the sands of time.

Introduction

Composing memorable quotes is probably civilization's oldest intellectual hobby that today is still bubbling away merrily with inexhaustible vigor and vitality. It is a favorite pastime of some of civilization's greatest—and least—thinkers. It is an outstanding way to distinguish yourself in society.

These gold nuggets of thought are super concentrated sayings: they range from the truly profound to the glibly humorous. But most (like mankind itself) fall somewhere between these two extremes. But all express a penetrating truth in a unique but easily understood form. Their grasp of the essence of our lives rings the proverbial bell in our minds.

Such gems of wisdom greatly predate Stone Age man's desire to express himself by painting on cave walls, an age-old attempt to capture, solidify and imprison on a time-surviving surface fleeting ideas and impressions.

Since the dawn of memory, mankind has been constantly seeking ways and means to immortalize those wisdoms that preserve his life, protect him from his dangerous surroundings, show him how to enjoy the pleasures of his world, and give him a stiff boost upwards and forwards in feeling equal to his superiors and arrogantly superior to his inferiors.

In another sense, aphorisms are part and parcel of mankind's endless search for eternal verities, those truths which expand knowledge of the present world and hopefully of the world to come. They are an educating heritage passed on from generation to generation.

Such sayings have always been, and will probably always remain, vastly popular. There is apparently no end to creating them.

Check with that endangered species, your local librarian, or better yet with her electronic replacement. Open any search engine on the Internet and type in the word "aphorisms." You will be flooded with titles of books dedicated to them, including entire encyclopedias and thesauruses. Bartlett's has become a byword.

On the lighter side, a compilation of clones of Murphy's Law manages to inject enough bitter humor and subtle charm to please anyone taking pleasure in the misery and/or discomfort of others. What the German's call "Schadenfreude"—malicious pleasure.

(Murphy's famous Law: "Anything that can go wrong, will go wrong" has been expanded by others to: "If anything can go wrong, it will go wrong, and at the worst possible time.")

Probably the first ones dealt with self-defence: "Wooden club and sharp stone make good weapons" and "Fire makes meat tastier" and so on.

Probably then came the more normal, but today considered outrageously chauvinist, "Dragging woman by hair to bed teaches her man is boss; she feels secure, that her man cares about her."

Even today, American rednecks are rumored to still have a futile ambition: To keep their wives in good spirits, they say: "Happy wife must feel that things could be much worse. So, keep wife pregnant in hot, humid summer and barefoot in cold, wet winter."

Modern historians credit Hippocrates, the father of modern medicine who wrote brief statements on health, with founding this art form. But undoubtedly, they were well developed in the pre-Greek civilizations, especially in the Far East.

Formulating these proven guidelines to life out of one's own mind is an art form bound only by the restrictions of clarity, insight and brevity.

As Shakespeare wrote in Hamlet almost half a millenium ago: "Brevity is the soul of wit."

Most persons prefer to call them aphorisms, although they have many other names. (See Appendix A.)

But just as many instinctively call them "wisdoms", a good old fashioned Anglo-Saxon word, in preference to its ancient Greek root, "aphorismos."

Definitions

Webster's dictionary defines an aphorism as "a concise statement of a principle, a terse formulation of a truth or sentiment, an adage;" while the Oxford calls them "any pithily expressed precept or observation; a maxim."

In short, aphorisms are uniquely phrased wisdoms ("aphorized" by an "aphorist") that cast penetrating glimpses into mankind's incestuous foibles, genetic stupidities and once-a-century wisdoms. Every people has such guidelines polished by generation after generation until they develop a rich patina. All such expressions, no matter their source, have several things in common:

They are all easily remembered and easily quoted—some so much so that they have become boring cliches losing both their beauty and their ability to surprise and instruct. For their very mention has a tendency to turn off the brain's capacity to absorb them. Yet, even if they have lost their effectiveness as life-pointers tested and retested by experience among jaded adults, they still influence youngsters who toss them back in the face of their parents as part of their rebellion against the mess these parents left them as an heritage.

In our most impressionable youth we all had drummed into our ears and brains many sharp expressions which today, as so-called wise adults, we quote, or have quoted at us, as we go about our daily lives. They are a living part of our culture. For example: "No news is good news" or "Where there's smoke, there's fire." (See Annex 2 for a short list.)

Many have become specialized sayings for certain sections of our lives, like "The life you save may be your own" for the driving public, while the military has coined such expressions as "On the ball, or on the boat," or "Be bright-eyed and bushy tailed."

They have withstood the erosion of both the horrors and joys of present times, of time itself. So far.

All aphorisms have one thing in common. If their contents are firmly grasped, they form long-lasting building blocks in our storehouse of conscious knowledge. They are treasures of the world's basic folklore.

Anyone seriously internalizing a goodly chunk of these power-packed sayings has acquired the knowledge of several doctorates in the science of understanding.

Writing them as a hobby indicates that you are on the road to acquiring several post doctorates. Writing memorable ones means you possess the wisdom to teach many a Ph.D. doing post graduate work.

(You can always buy an impressively framed Ph.D. diploma on the Internet to substantiate your claim of being educated. Has anyone ever challenged any diploma on any wall? Who cares if the non-accredited university with an impressive name issuing such doctorates consists, as a rule, of a post office box rented by a local printer.)

Knowledge is accepted blindly on the basis of a certificate, not on the basis of performance.

But absorbing aphorisms requires more than a hasty glance at each one. They must be reflectively savored and thoughtfully digested mentally, emotionally, until their message adheres to your personality. For example: "You only live once."

Any normal person with a contemplative mind can busy himself for minutes, hours, and days in trying to understand all the implications of these few simple words. Does it mean you should live life to the hilt without giving a damn for others, or should you always keep peeking at the Pearly Gates from the corner of your eyes?

Mulling over such short sayings will often undermine many deeply rooted conceptions. Often they open the porthole of your mind to a startling view on commonly accepted beliefs and ideas; they can be healthy icon smashers, upsetting the smug apple cart in your mind. Some persons get a boost by thinking deeply about those that complement their present lifestyles; others need strange ideas that shock their comfortable beliefs and sensibilities.

Each individual has a different capacity for "deep" absorption. Some can barely manage to internalize one each day. Others can easily digest a handful. Some grasp the full import immediately; others must chew slowly until their mental enzymes flow to digest them. Still others must read and reread them several times before they build a solid foundation.

Poetry's Little Brother

Although somewhat akin to poetry, the differences are great. Poems often follow definite, rigid patterns. They may run in length from ultra-short to so endlessly long that their beauty must be inhaled in measured doses.

In contrast, most aphorisms are condensed into one sentence. Poems may have many ideas; aphorisms generally have only one. Both poetry and aphorisms seek beauty in words. But in aphorisms the clarity of the idea expressed takes precedent over all other things. If you reread an aphorism, it should not be to better understand it, but mainly to appreciate its emotional and mental impact.

Writing a poem may entail a long period of brain torture. The self-inflicted pain in crystallizing an aphorism may be just as intense, but it consumes much less time. But the joy of accomplishment may be just as great, if not greater, since you will probably compose many more aphorisms than poems.

Nevertheless, much poetry, especially in vintage theatre plays, gives birth to phrases that stand alone:

"All the world's a stage, and all the men and women merely players."
William Shakespeare

"Art is long, life is short."
Johann Wolfgang von Goethe

"Never send to know for whom the bell tolls, it tolls for thee."
John Donne

"This above all: to thine own self be true.
And it must follow, as the night the day,
Thou canst not then be false to any man."
William Shakespeare

But the most famous sayings are one-liners that stand alone.

"Work expands to fill the time available for its completion."
Prof. C. Northcote Parkinson

"One ad is worth more to a newspaper than forty editorials."
Will Rogers.

Of course, Will Roger's "All I know is what I read in the newspapers" has grown and grown. It now encompasses the crushing and destructive burden of modern media: the radio, TV, and Internet, and so on. Still the old-fashioned neighborhood gossip "klatsch" in the local beauty shop has not only managed to hold its own, but has grown and thrived since the present generation has abandoned Biblical morality for sexual sophistication: Modern women have much more time to "fulfil" themselves with acts of modern "freedom", once known as deadly sins leading straight to the burning pits of Hell.

One of Will Rogers sayings which needs no updating is: "I don't make jokes. I just watch the government and report the facts."

Who has not been stirred—and cannot quote—such phrases as:

"The only thing we have to fear is fear itself."
Franklin D. Roosevelt

"Ask not what your country can do for you, ask what you can do for your country."
John F. Kennedy

"I have a dream, that one day on the red hills of Georgia, the sons of former slaves and the sons of former slave owners will be able to sit down together at the table of brotherhood."
Martin Luther King Jr.

"There are three kinds of lies—lies, damned lies, and statistics."
Mark Twain

Who has not been activated into motion by such Chinese folk sayings as "The longest journey starts with a single step."? How many of us have been told that "One picture is worth ten thousand words."?

Yiddish, a bastardized derivation (dialect) of High German, is rich in them. "Love is sweet, but tastes best with bread."

The Bible calls them proverbs.

"Greater love hath no man than this, that a man lay down his life for his friends."
John 15.13

"Dust thou art, and until dust shall thou return."
Genesis 3.19

But on the whole, modern aphorisms have replaced Biblical proverbs.

But these generally lack a true religious element—unless you care to replace God with Science and His prophets with Scientists in White, who, incidentally include all too many grubby-minded persons hoodwinking the public while perpetually undermining each other in the guise of scientific progress and personal integrity.

Personality of Writers

Wisdoms can be composed—to repeat a ubiquitous cliche thrown out at every sign of discrimination—by all ranks and files of society, regardless of race, color, religion, ethnic background, sex, sexual proclivities and perversions, such as sadism and masochism, and psychiatric behavior such as borderline insanity, wife battering, incest, pedophilia, sodomy, pederasty, and so on.

Creators of such brilliant sayings range from downtrodden humble, illiterate hoboes with a high degree of intelligence, to humorless hippies rejecting the blessings of civilization. These latter self-styled searchers for salvation wander romantically to far distant, esoteric green pastures, to find scintillating savants with immense stores of abstract and impractical fifth-hand knowledge which is so old that it seems futuristic. These "gatekeepers" to the inner world find it hard to make a living unless they are blessed with both a hearty dose of sincerity, charlatanism and charisma.

Some of the best—and some of the most disgusting—are graffiti scribbled on the sides of walls of buildings. New York is infamous for its decorated subway trains. For example:

"God is dead."
Nietzsche

Responded some witty commuter:

"Nietzsche is dead."
God

We will spare readers the toilet-wall scribblings by budding, ripe and decaying sexual perverts.

But all these writers, no matter their background, have one common salient feature: they are keen observers of the human comedy.

They have a peculiar way of looking at things. This is the secret of their success.

They clearly spot and isolate those indistinct entities most of us sense only vaguely through a murky cloud. But once they formulate their "visions", the entire picture literally jumps into focus.

Some are critical onlookers at this circus, offering the advice of armchair savants and generals; some are active participants, wheelers and dealers, playing (or at least trying to play) a vital role as events unfold before they very eyes.

Homosexuals, for some unexplained reason (science has produced more unsubstantiated theories than facts) are a rich source, out of all proportion to their percentage in society, even much above their boasted (and exaggerated) percentage in society.

Perhaps homos, being closeted somewhat from the mainstream society for generations, visualize things from a different angle.

It will be interesting to see, now that so many homos have come slinking nervously or bouncing arrogantly out of the closet, if they will lose their lopsided gift to produce glib wisecracks and/or deep profundities. If so, it will be a terrible shame.

For the betterment of our culture we should chase them all back deep, deep into the closet where they can again contribute more to the general insight. Leaving them run free might dissipate exceptional gifts of another Oscar Wilde who wrote: "The public is wonderfully tolerant. It forgives everything except genius."

Of course, this was not exactly true. The public applauded (and still applauds) the genius of Wilde; it just looked askance at his sexual inclinations, which have since become accepted practice between consenting adults and underage minors.

Surprisingly, the overwhelming majority of writers are men. The paucity of women writers is a mystery. That their efforts died still-born due to male opposition is nonsense. Western women have written, and are still writing, great literature.

(But then there are other fields where the longevity sex has made few major contributions, where it lags far behind the accomplishments of its menfolk. What woman has written great classical music? Beat men at chess?)

Among the few notable feminine exceptions at bitter barbs was the late Dorothy Rothschild Parker, who added spice to New York City's famed Algonquian Round Table.

Several of her witticisms typified the American experience.

"The only "ism" Hollywood believes in is plagiarism," and "This is not a novel to be tossed aside lightly. It should be thrown with great force."

Another one credited to her (which has not found its way into popular collections) is "There is plenty of money around. It just isn't in the right pockets."

Epiphany

Aphorisms and poetry do have one thing in common. Both stem from a literary epiphany—a brilliant manifestation of awareness, of reality, of truth, of beauty, ranging from transcendental spirituality to down-to-earth common sense.

These epiphanies strike at odd times: in that pre-sleep or pre-awakening blurred zone when the mind slithers from hazy subconsciousness to clear consciousness. Then mental and logic short circuits apparently occur in the brain.

Another fertile time is while dreaming or lost in reveries and fantasies, or in that split second upon awakening when trying to recall those brightly colored dreams and irrational thoughts which plagued or comforted you during the night. Learn to rekindle your dreams.

And they occur, of course, while walking, and back and forth pacing. Some persons find the slightly jolting of a car, bus, train, ship, or plane ignites their brain, while others need the quiet of sitting at their desk when their mind strays from their work in pursuit of an orgasmic sexual encounter.

Two fruitful sources for men are singing in the shower or shaving. Apparently, the stinging impact of a needle stream on the skin shocks the brain, or the sight of one's own face in the mirror taps either a well of inspiration or desperation. Both give birth to thoughts of "what might have been."

Women often receive sparks of inspiration while putting on makeup. Then their mind slithers into capturing that captivating, handsome, thrilling, romantic, sexy, sophisticated, charismatic, wealthy (and so and so on) stranger who exists only in the fermenting fantasies of hack writers of cheap romances.

Where do these epiphanies come from? Obviously from the depths of your frenetic subconscious or from some submerged layer of your memory. Mine these wisps of whispers that float around in your brain.

Capturing Them

Epiphanies must be imprisoned immediately on paper or dictated into a tape. You may also wake in the night with an aphorism trailing out of a fading dream. A joint pen/flashlight is invaluable if you want to abstain from wakening your spouse by turning on the light, for they possess the cruel characteristic of flitting with electronic speed from your memory. The very brightness of their brilliance deceives you into believing that they are etched deeply into your memory cells. Nothing could be further from the truth. Like lightning they come and like thieves in the night they melt silently away, leaving you with only a tantalizing memory of having lost something great. But if one gets away, don't give up hope. Often they return in ten year cycles.

It is an excellent idea to anchor in detail the peculiarity of an idea as soon as possible. All too often the special essence of an idea is meaningless in a scribbled note.

Why scribbled? Because you were afraid if you wrote slowly, legibly, the idea would fade before you put it down on paper.

Connecting thoughts are missing. So, rewrite and expand on your scribbling as soon as possible. But if you can't decipher your scrawled gibberish, reading your notes again and again may restore their originality. Although it may now seem to have lost its unique creativity brilliance, it is still a good idea—at least it will outrank those pontificated by politicians and preachers.

Some of their faded brilliance may be attributed to the fact that they are no longer new to you. Also, you wisely may have had second thoughts.

Keep a secret journal of your thoughts. It is also a good idea to make in-depth notes on all aspects of your life. It will help you to clarify yourself. Let yourself go in your secret journal. Write down your innermost, suppressed thoughts: Is your marriage on the rocks? Do you suspect your spouse of cheating? And so on.

At the very least, it will often make pleasant reading in your old age when you comment inwardly:

"What a genius I was then," although now and then you feel you should be saying, "What an asshole."

Hobby

Writing aphorisms can become a marvelous hobby, a method of getting even with the world or slyly jabbing at a friend or an enemy. They are a relaxing form of creative writing, a sort of mental chess played on a multicolored chessboard with differently sized squares and even an occasional circle.

Their composition can be a pastime just as amusing and as engrossing as crossword puzzles, bridge, chess, kibitzing, as refreshing as meditation or as stimulating as fighting with one's spouse, or striving to outwit an author by pinpointing the "villain" in a detective story.

Composing these concise sayings easily outshines all of these other games since they sharpen your grasp of ideas, of people, of events, of situations, of the world itself which engulfs, and often smothers, each one of us daily with its mishmash of illusions and/or realities.

Understanding our topsy-turvy surroundings might not increase your chances of making more money, but it will help you develop a philosophical attitude to explain your relative middle-class poverty. At any rate, no one has yet founded a sub-sub-specialty to diagnose any new disease inflicted by writing or reading aphorisms.

Here is your chance to indulge in a bit of creative writing. Who knows? Perhaps even a bit of creative thinking that future generations will appreciate.

This hobby is particularly fitting for elderly persons, for septuagenarians, for octogenarians, especially those who feel a creeping mental blurring due to their advancing age, and suffer from an ever-shortening attention span. Fatigued, long-winded poets can find their salvation here.

You can compose them everywhere and anytime, at home, at work, traveling to work, caught in an exasperating traffic jam. No need to even take both hands off the wheel to write if you have a small tape.

It is a relaxing hobby. Why build up tension leading to a heart attack or stroke, if you can relax and soothe your nerves while juggling your thoughts?

It is an unending journey in self-exploration. Your subconscious will sprout astonishing feelings and objectionable beliefs from the inner recesses of your mind. Freeing your subconscious is a strong catharsis. You will surprise yourself by facing the truth.

Some spouses may even begin to better understand their counter-parts. ("The shortest journey to the bedroom starts with one kiss and/or compliment.") It may also give you a better insight into the jittery world of your family and friends, of causes, ideologies, and so on.

Your vague opinions become focussed.

You might have always considered yourself a liberal, but as you dig deeper into your thoughts, as you peel away layer after layer of your brainwashing, you may discover you are a solid conservative; or an idealistic radical longing to go out and demonstrate, but violently, yet you are too cowardly to follow through.

Aren't all "isms" (liberalism, conservatism, radicalism, and so on), all too often a function of your age and your slippery little niche in history?

Who knows? You might even become a better person. You certainly will become more alert to your inner personality and to the outer world, especially to its dangers and joys.

After reading this mini-primer so far, you have come to one of sev-eral conclusions:

This hobby is not for you, or that it definitely is since you have already written, or thought of, a few or many aphorisms, and you would like to step up your production considerably.

If the latter, you will shortly come to the conclusion that you have run out of ideas.

Creative Block

What happens if your spontaneous output dies? If your fountain of ideas runs dry? If your well of inspiration actually dries up? If your mind goes blank? This can be really worrying if you have made writing aphorisms into a pet hobby.

You try to define the problem.

The first suspicion that may sneak into your mind is that you have used up your inventory of original ideas. This is highly doubtful. (Some middle-aged persons even develop a suspicion that this is their first inklings of Alzheimer's, despite the widely held belief that a sure sign of this disease is a person's unawareness of this condition.)

Others might even begin to search desperately for a solution by reading articles on "writer's block", of writers who moan and groan about staring at that flickering monitor screen, or at that blank piece of paper in their typewriter. Some even claim that the sight of their tape recorder drives them speechless; others fall into the habit of nervously tapping their fingers relentlessly on their desk, drinking endless cups of strong coffee, or chain smoking. All this, of course, is nothing more than a bout of self-pity generated by self-doubt.

Don't worry, even the best soil should lie fallow now and then to regain its vigor. Just accept the fact that your mind needs nourishment, or perhaps only priming, to overcome a barren period—or perhaps it is only slowly gestating.

Another barrier is that many of us have room in our heads for only one serious thought at a time. This thought can lie there, acting as a mental barrier, preventing another serious thought from roosting there, developing, and reaching maturity in your mind.

Once captured on paper or tape, the brain is cleared to become fertile soil for new ideas to take root and flower. Often the new idea is a development of the previous one; sometimes it has no logical or emotional connection.

Simply writing down words on paper often generates new ideas. Rewriting sparks the generating process to tap new layers of imagination.

Your mind should be a moving assembly belt, not a locked bank vault. Moreover, some of us fear (for some strange reason) that once you express your "great thought", it will be your last original one.

Nothing is further from the truth. You will give birth again and again.

Several more possibilities exist to jump start your inspirational pump. Don't be afraid they will cause that cursed and/or blessed disease called "writer's diarrhea", often a precursor to writer's dysentery.

There may be many reasons for your dry period.

Probably the primary reason is a lack of mental energy due to emotional stagnation reinforced by plain old-fashioned laziness.

Let us tackle these two problems separately, although they are often closely interwoven.

Perhaps you are over reacting emotionally to certain events in your life. Some personal emotional problem or problems are draining your mental energies, willingly or unwillingly. You are trapped into tunnel vision unable to see the distant and blessed light at the end of the tunnel; often your problem becomes a continuousl chant in your mind, a sort of an 'idée fixe'.

As a rule, these blocks are caused by a few main paralyzing emotions, specifically those ancient life-long, live-in, continuously quarreling partners called love and hate,

Let's not forget that although love and hate can blow a fuse in your brain, they can also inspire you. But both limit the range of your enthusiasm by self-centered concentration. The lovesick often find themselves writing love poems. As a rule, they are very bad poems. You may not think so at first, not even 20–30 years later, when you accidentally find them. You will be too overwhelmed with a flood of nostalgic memories to value their worth.

Love can thrill you and cause you to visualize yourself as a hero; your mind is adrift, with ideas and longings and erotic day dreaming; you may even decide to reform yourself and turn over a new leaf. Something like a New Year's Resolution made with the firmest of intentions and broken at the first weak moment—a few days later. Definitely before New Year's Eve.

Hate may force you to focus all your thoughts on committing the perfect murder.

Don't let the authorities scare you: there are murders so perfect that nobody even suspects they took place. Probably, a goodly number are committed by those close to the authorities.

These two emotional blocks can be strangled out of existence by various means.

Love?

Take a sex cure. Get as much sex as you can bear, wherever and whenever you can. In the era of liberated women, there are plenty of sensible women out there, not yet ready to settle down and turn "conventional" in the old-fashioned meaning of the word, who will supply your needs. Without any thought of entrapment.

All they want in return is some sincere flattery topped off by a good candlelight dinner with a bottle of wine with a vintage (real or faked) label. If you can't stomach wine, some fabulous orchids may have the same intoxicating effect. Season the evening with soft, romantic music to taste.

It helps to sprinkle your conversation with such blarney as love, affection, adorable, soul mates, at last I've found you, where have you been all my life? How young you look (you can never say this too often to a woman if you say it in different formats), and so on. Most liberated women seek "romance", not love. Love entails obligations.

They only want a chance to live for the moment like their soap opera heroines; also, they want to preen themselves before their less fortunate and envious sisters.

But be wary of free love; it can be bankruptingly expensive.

And if you can't find such a woman, there are plenty of prostitutes whose profession is to relieve sexual pressures for a fair price. An older whore might not awaken youthful visions, but she will certainly drain you expertly.

You will be surprised how sexual excursions of any type will dilute your focus on your true love.

As for lovesick women, getting laid is much easier. And the man will pay, and pay, and pay. He will even feel like a hero.

Hate? Take a hate cure. Check around for some object upon which to vent your hate, until the hatred within you is (almost) expended.

But suppose you are a mild sort of a person and can't find something or somebody to hate? A good bet is to closely examine your religious or political beliefs with critical eyes. List all its promises and its failures. Then, blame its failures on any other person with the same religion or political beliefs, a person who "corrupts" the system.

Alternatively, you can vent your hate on believers in any other religion or political beliefs.

It is always so easy to find a good excuse to hate and love.

One thing seems certain: a man or a woman in love rarely can spare the inspiration to hate at the same time—unless he/she has fallen into the trap of falling in love with a hateful person. Then he/she begins to despise himself. Does this happen only in fiction?

Other Blocks to Creativity

It might also be a good idea to see if your mind is not semi-paralyzed by one of the following that can dull your senses with "moods" and "brooding."

The list is rather long (yet far from complete) since some of us need to define a specific angle of a generality:

- Despair and/or depression
- Vague, undefined fears called anxieties
- Panic, specific fears, worrying
- Disappointments
- Pessimism
- Resentment
- Fear of failure, present and future
- Frustrations
- Butterfly thinking
- Putting off things and letting things pile up until they become mental burdens blocking other thoughts, i.e., actual laziness creates laziness
- Accumulating mental garbage
- Stymied by trying to attain unobtainable perfection
- Taking things to heart
- Fighting for lost causes
- Comparing yourself to others, often to many others at the same time, and developing an inferiority complex.
- Waiting for the right time, place and atmosphere for inspira-tion
- Lack of appreciation, response, rewards, self-esteem, self-worth, self-accomplishment
- Fear of competition
- Lack of priorities
- Not taking the first step

Energy Gainers to Step Up Production

- Good physical condition
- Proper diet, exercise, sleep
- Enjoying conflict and outwitting competition
- Concentrating on one thing and avoiding butterfly thinking
- Using a warming up gambit
- Break huge projects down into small ones and tackle the smaller one step at a time; this makes it seem easier
- Setting goals and trapping yourself into accepting deadlines
- Avoiding distracting temptations, such as TV, radio, reading, etc.
- Actual progress will generate enthusiasm to continue
- Self-stimulation and self-inspiration through: listing and thinking of rewards, becoming aware of the successes of others
- Recalling past and present successes and rewards
- Positive mental attitude, enthusiasm, self-esteem, courage, pride
- Augments and debates
- Recharging batteries through receiving praise, appreciation and interest from others
- Ability to show off
- Learning from disappointments, set backs, negative emotions
- Belief in future
- Going ahead full steam by ignoring emotions—wonderful, if you can do this
- Sublimate the energy you are wasting on your problems into productive channels

Getting Ideas

Once you have recharged your batteries, the next step is to get ideas.

Arguments are often wonderful stimulants; especially heated ones where you maintain control with clenched thoughts, or when you lose control and your tongue lashes out wildly (before the censor of emotion or the critic of logic imposes silence by ordering: Shut up, you fool.)

Your adrenaline roars forth, preparing you for fight or flight. Latent ideas, words, and connections burst the barriers of rigid control where they have been banished for logical or illogical reasons. Their explosion astonishes both yourself and your antagonist.

This spontaneous reaction somewhat resembles an automatic curse, but on a somewhat higher intellectual level. All too often, however, you regret (or you should) your outburst. Sooner or later you will have to apologize.

Train yourself to say "I'm sorry" as soon as possible. Delay makes apologizing twice as hard.

Try brain picking others for opinions by utilizing spontaneous interviews. Do this with anybody who will inspire your emotional or logical reaction. Usually your best sources are those who disagree with you. Or you can read watered down versions of books on philosophy, history, religion, and science.

If this doesn't work, ask yourself: what can I criticize in the public speeches, articles, books, political platforms, election promises, planning objectives, financing and especially in generally accepted beliefs?

Nothing and nobody are perfect.

You can always find something to criticize—and rightly so—in everything and everybody. A person only 90 per cent right can be ridiculed and crushed by concentrating on the false ten per cent. Every genius has his Achilles Heel. The most that can be said for most persons of enormous talent is that they lay the foundations for further improvements by others. This holds true for such mental giants as Einstein, Freud, Marx and Darwin.

Another way to stimulate your inspiration is to get out of your mental rut. Meet and listen to new and exciting people; people bursting with ideas and energy, people who have something startling or unconventional to say.

The Internet is bustling with frustrated persons looking for kindred souls so they can compare and enjoy each other's miseries. Sorrow and misery like company.

So what if they are neurotics? Cracked persons often are terribly interesting. But beware of marriage and "we are soul mates who have finally found each other" traps some instinctively try to set. Most new friends on the Internet should stay friends on the Internet, as far away as possible, yet as close as tapping on a few keys.

But now and then the Internet spawns up intelligent persons with dull spouses looking for a life raft of hope in the vast ocean of lost souls.

We've seen people in a picture gallery become wildly enthusiastic, almost orgasmic, at a splash of color, at a crooked line, at a hazy landscape, at a lopsided, primitive painting that looks like the work of a dull third-grader, or viewing hard pornography disguised as "Holy Art" on the Internet.

Some persons are jarred into a burst of inspiration when they leave their routine surroundings, especially when on vacation far away from their daily scramble to make a living.

Their imaginations are rekindled by the majesty of their surroundings: distant snowy mountains, endless forests, the serene pounding of waves, a violent and sudden thunder storm, burning desert sands, or the blazing glory of the autumn leaves.

Any monumental man-made impressive sight, even though it destroys the pristine beauty of nature, like the pyramids, the skyscrapers, the Golden Gate Bridge, and so on, will send some persons into raptures.

If you can't get away, try exploring nearby sites. Views and places you consider commonplace all too often give strangers an uplift. Find out why. Jettison your jaded, blasé outlook. See familiar things through the eyes of an eager tourist.

Another anomaly of the human mind is the wine cult. Some so-called connoisseurs tasting a rare wine will go into raptures, although they honestly don't have the slightest feel for any wine.

Drinking alcohol in its various forms constitutes a special problem. Some find that a drink or two stimulates their minds into belching forth witty jewels, but others (especially women) find that alcohol also casts a mist between their ability to differentiate between true grandeur and fool's gold.

What might seem startling as the alcohol percolates through your brain, generally becomes puerile after the fog in your mind fades. After all, you are not trying to inspire other drunks? Or are you?

Yet there have been plenty of confirmed alcoholics who have written enchanting poetry and great books. You'll be surprised how many.

You can never know about alcohol until you try. One thing is certain. A drink a day is good for your spirits and heart; heavy drinking can lead to cirrhosis of the liver, wife battering, and becoming somebody's daylight nightmare.

We have yet to hear of any user of hard or soft drugs producing hard ideas.

But coffee, and to a lesser extent tea and cola, seem to add a bit of pep to a tired brain.

Another method of goading the muse to life should be mentioned. Fetishism.

Many writers need the inspiration of what can be best described as a "fetish" to put their creative abilities in gear. For example, Frederich von Schiller, German dramatist, poet and writer, used to sniff the aroma (?) of rotten apples. The list of writers who needed strange shots in the brain is long, ranging from soaking in a hot bath to listening to the same musical composition over and over.

Emotional Status When Composing

Now, determine what triggers in your mind an emotional, mental or logical response. (Doesn't emotion always precede logic?)

Are you usually calm and collected, but this time you are furious with clenched hands and with eyes fixed on someone's jugular vein, thirsting for the taste of fresh blood?

What mood best energizes you to action? When you are:
❐ Angry at injustice
❐ Feeling exploited
❐ Reacting to insults
❐ Aggressive and argumentative
❐ Infuriated and/or outraged
❐ Bitter and/or cranky
❐ Enjoying a rare burst of moral courage
❐ Enthusiastic
❐ Thoughtful
❐ Resentful

notes:

Your Most Creative Periods

What period of the day helps jar your mind into functioning at super gear?

Is it daybreak, broad daylight, sunset, twilight, nightfall, night, midnight when shadows of ghosts go suddenly and inexplicably "bump" in the placid void of hellish, cosmic and endless darkness? Are you a morning lark who comes instinctively wide awake when the sun peeps over the horizon (despite drawn curtains and total darkness); or are you a midnight owl with piercing eyes praying for prey? Exploit the delicate, cyclic rhythms of your personal life.

Which physical activity stimulates your brain: driving, jogging, pacing up and down, swimming, eating, shaving, showering, smoking, dressing, putting on make up to hide the ravages of the years, sipping a cup of hot, steamy coffee, or taking a sly and secret shot of early morning bourbon?

To create successful aphorisms you must feel intensely about something, anything, past, present or future. Try to recall your emotion at some high peak in your life, a moment whose emotional intensity engraved your brain, either for good or for evil. If you can recreate that invigorating and inspiring feeling, you are indeed lucky.

Refurbishing

Firstly, let us try to refurbish your brain cells by rereading your most successful aphorisms. Inspiration often comes from patting yourself on the back. (It is much more encouraging, of course, if someone you admire does the patting.)

Alternatively, reading great aphorisms written by the masters may restore your inspirational energies. But be careful. Don't let their brilliance intimidate you into silent paralysis. Some have germinated for years both mentally and on paper. They may have run through many versions.

You are only reading the tip of the writer's iceberg. Time has caused his bad ones to gradually fade away. Sometimes the writer may have even judiciously suppressed them.

Thus, never be ashamed of your bad ones. Time will bury them, unless you have a vigorous enemy with a festering grudge. Your problem is to disseminate your good ones and to keep them alive before an appreciative public.

Study the Masters

Don't only read the masters, but also study them.

You have already taken a first stride when you worked for your "doctorate."

Read now not only for content, but also to try to capture and learn the masters personal process of composition.

Until you finish reading the following suggestions, put the idea of composing your own original aphorisms on a far back burner. Of course, if an aphorism sneaks slyly, fully polished into your mind, welcome and lasso it.

The great contributors in any field; music, literature, poetry, philosophy, math, chess, and so on, might have been born with huge natural gifts, yet they all had to upgrade this talent to genius by studying and absorbing the methods of their predecessor who laid the solid foundations of their art.

So, you must grasp and internalize the basis of any art. These methods, these foundations, are needed since you must gear yourself to the mind of your readers so they can easily absorb your ideas.

But don't skim over those you like with a chuckle and/or mental nod of agreement, and shake your head in disapproval at those that irritate you. Analyze them structurally.

Tear them to pieces. Dig deeper into them before accepting any as the pleasant or unpleasant gospel truth. Test each one against your own store of knowledge and experience.

Ask yourself:

- Why do I like (or dislike) this slice of life?
- What gives it its charm?
- What gives it its insight?
- Why do I instinctively recognize it as true?
- Is it really true or just a clever play on words and ideas?
- Is it a short-lived gimmick, a passing fad?
- Do they use enticing words that sidetrack you slightly from their meaning?
- What motivated the writer?
- What was his aim?
- What are its consequences and ramifications?
- Why haven't I thought of this myself?
- Are there layers of meaning here, each layer indicating some thing else?
- What latent knowledge in my mind has it tapped?
- Are they long-winded or short and forceful?
- Do they contain shifts in thinking? Do they entice your thoughts in one direction and then suddenly divert your mind in another, surprising direction?

Keep this list of analytic thought joggers in mind, for it will come in handy when you are judging your own brain bastards.

Here is an example of a superficial analysis: Ben Franklin wrote: "There are more old drunkards than old doctors."

Is this really true or just an excuse for tying one on? What other questions can you ask about Good Olde Ben's saying?

notes:

Rewriting the Masters

Let us now tackle other methods to prime the mental pump. Although priming inspiration seems like a contradiction in terms, it often works—but not always. Sometimes the mental well is a dry water hole in a lifeless, barren desert.

Even when it works, when the well is bubbling full, inspiration is often a tricky imp to corner; often when cornered impossible to harness, and when harnessed he may be as balky as a Missouri mule. Nevertheless, it is worth an energetic try, if just for practice.

Doesn't "Practice make perfect"?

Try to improve on well-known aphorisms by rewriting them. Even if you find them perfect, try updating any style and antique language by substituting modern nouns, verbs, adjectives.

But be careful. Sometimes modification will desecrate their charm.

"Spoil the rod and spoil the child" can become a prosaic, dull and bureaucratic, "A hearty spanking will prevent the child from going chaotic."

This so-called improvement lacks the sparkle of a phrase that has engraved a pattern in our brain cells.

Ralph Waldo Emerson wrote, "If a man has a genius for painting, poetry, music, architecture, or philosophy, he makes a bad husband, and an ill provider."

The same idea is expressed much briefer in this rewritten version: "A genius in painting, poetry, music, architecture or philosophy makes a bad husband and an ill provider."

Has the rewrite robbed the saying of its impact and charm?

Notice that the first version has 22 words, the second only 17. (See the chapter on Polishing for a tested method of reducing wordiness.)

Rewrite the basic ideas in the space provided.

"If all blondes are considered dumb, why do so many brunettes bleach their hair? Are smart men looking for dumb blondes?

"Not all women belong in a kitchen, but every women should learn to whip up a delicious concoction in the Master's bedroom."

"Every family must have a boss; partnerships in couples work best if the feminine partner smiles in adoration."

Here are some really difficult ones to rewrite:

"There are only two truly infinite things, the universe and stupidity. And I am not so sure about the universe." Albert Einstein

"Rich bachelors should be heavily taxed. It is not fair that some men should be happier than others." Oscar Wilde

If you compare your rewrites with the brilliant originals, you may surprise yourself. Yours might be better, even much better, especially if the original has lost some of its glamour due to nuance changes in English.

If your rephrasing actually improves a few, you will certainly get a boost if your friends truly find your version outshines the original.

Who knows? They might compare you to such monumental figures as William Shakespeare, George Bernard Shaw, Oscar Wilde, Francois La Rochfoucauld, Johann Wolfgang von Goethe, Friedrich Wilhelm Nietzsche, George Christoph Lichtenberg, and so on.

If so, smile genially, but start eyeing with a suspicious wariness their opinions on all other subjects.

Changing Basic Meanings

Another method to regain inspiration is to compose aphorisms by simple variation and substitution. Changes can be made in the subject, object, intention, sequence of words, thought, time frame, speed, place, and so on. Additions and deletions can also prove especially useful if you want to expand or restrict the subject matter.

Eventually everything has been changed. Here is an easy example.

"But where are the snows of yesteryear?"
Francois Villon

You can easily replace the word "snows" with "loves" to get:

"But where are the loves of yesteryear?"

Some more substitutions for "snows" can be: hopes, dreams, friends, enemies, frustrations and so on.

What school child has not heard the saying: "All roads lead to Rome"

This short sentence is composed of four elements:

All
Roads
Lead to
Rome

Let us add only word to the above phrase, a word that changes its meaning entirely.

Thus, "Once all roads led to Rome."

Other substitutions for any of these four elements give us:

"All roads leave Rome."

"All cultures lead to Rome."

True, none of these variations has the same impact as the original "All roads lead to Rome."

Because the word "Rome" meant more than a city. It was a civilization. Rome was the focal point of a huge empire encompassing various peoples, cultures, and religions; it was the world center of trade, philosophy, education, culture, law and so on. Rome was the closest thing at that time to a global village.

Another variation: "All roads lead to God."

(It has been replaced by Paris for Americans; and New York for Frenchmen.)

If we remember that the Eternal City also housed sadistic citizens with an unquenchable thirst to feast their eyes and emotions on the blood of gladiators, we can formulate:

"Roman culture was steeped in poetry and blood."

Some More Examples

"It is better to have loved and lost than never to have loved at all" becomes "It is better to have loved and lost than to be hated and win."

Another variation on the same theme:

"Better for a woman to be married and divorced than never to have been married at all."

And why not: "Better a wife battered occasionally by her loving husband than a lonely spinster battered only by her longings and her thoughts of what might have been and/or lost opportunities."

"Work fascinates me; I can sit and watch people work for hours" becomes "Love fascinates me; I can save my life by waiting until the insanity of the sex trap passes."

"The road to hell is paved with good intentions."

Why not: "The road to heaven is paved with good deeds."

Or: "The road to success is paved with many failures."

We can easily develop the famous dictum describing the Communist brotherhood: "We are all equal but some of us are more equal than others."

Two versions based on the same illogical trap:

"We are all infallible but some of us are more infallible than others."

"We are all unique but some of us are more unique than others."

Another example: "Some of my best friends are Jews," becomes "Some of my best friends are anti-Semites."

Kipling wrote:

"Oh, East is East, and West is West
And never the twain shall meet."

More or less on the same scale we have:

"Love is love, and sex is sex,
And sometimes the twain do meet."

Or:

"Law is law, and justice is justice,
When will the twain meet?"

Here is an extreme example:

"Which came first, the chicken or the egg?" becomes "Which came first, God or man?"

In a lighter mood, let us take a generally accepted belief, namely, "All lawyers are thieving scoundrels."

Let's keep the word "lawyer" but find a substitute for "thieving scoundrels."

Here are several possible variations on this theme:

"Lawyers are licensed crooks."
"Lawyers are scoundrels with diplomas."
"Lawyers are legalized bloodsuckers/leeches."
"Lawyers, prostitutes and politicians are necessary evils."

Now most persons (except lawyers and sometimes their wives and/or their mistresses) will accept most of the viewpoints expressed above. This helps explain why members of this profession persistently try to avoid the term "lawyer" and prefer to call themselves with such dignified titles as advocates, counselor-at-law, attorney-at-law, and so on.

By using the term "counselor" they even shed responsibility for losing your case since they only advised you in a most ambiguous way. So, when things go wrong, they can point out that they also hinted at the opposite course of action—or inaction.

Lawyers are like lovers; you can't live with them and you can't live without them.

But let's leave our readers with a pleasant thought about lawyers:

"The first and last honest lawyer died of hunger."

Does anyone hear an echo of the famous saying: "The first and last Christian died on the cross?"

Reversing the Order

Everyone knows that a dog is man's best friend. The truth, of course, is the opposite. "Man is dog's best friend." Dogs realized thousands of years ago that hitchhiking a ride on mankind would improve tremendously their canine standard of living. A variation gives us: "A man is woman's best friend."

Translations

There is another possibility—translations. If you know any European foreign language, especially French, Spanish, Italian, German (all have contributed greatly to Anglo-Saxon culture) try translating little known ones into hard-hitting English. Or grasp the basic essence and formulate it in your own words.

A comprehensive bilingual pocket dictionary is a dire necessity even if you are truly bilingual.

Changing Yourself

As noted earlier, all aphorisms (good, bad or indifferent) charm us by casting a particular insight, one might say a peculiar peek, into the chaotic zigzagging of the human brain.

So, if we don't have this specific insight, perhaps you can develop it from our submerged dormant potentialities.

But this, first of all, requires making a courageous and often painful look at yourself and defining various aspects of your personality. This soul-searching striptease might even persuade you to change both your deeply ingrained perspective and your field of observation.

Soul searching helps us break out of our mental rut, helps to shake our minds free from both its "black and white" one-sided tract thinking, and also from the effects of a life-long brainwashing (generally unintentional) inflicted on us by our parents, schooling, friends, enemies, spouses, work, society, our country.

All of these entities sincerely believe they are only doing "what is best" for us by inflicting on us their solutions to problems formulated from their life, religion, loyalties, failures, successes, and traditional objects of hate and love.

(So many people are so unselfishly trying to help us see the "right way", i.e., their way. They try to convince all others that they are right, that all others are wrong.)

Of course, persuading others helps them to convince themselves, helps them to overcome their own doubts. There must be a psychiatric definition for this perversion. Some missionaries have made their doubts their guiding light to the truth.

There are several small, but to some of us excruciating, exercises to help you lift anchor from your past and present, and reorient yourself differently. The following self-quizzes should help you change your way of visualizing things by simply adopting a new personality, a pseudo personality—if only for a short time. You may be shocked at seeing yourself in your mental and emotional nude.

Reorientation requires clambering up from the placid plane of your daily life of boredom to a (more or less) slippery and stormy summit. You must not only abandon your daily routine and prosaic life, but also see the same world with fresh eyes.

Don't fear quitting your comfortable and safe rut. In all likelihood, you probably will become so adjusted to your new outlook that it will also become a pleasant rut. But at least it should be a shallower one, allowing you to jump easier into another rut. Even if you fail to acquire a facility to produce aphorisms by changing your approach, you will (hopefully) enjoy the vigor of a deeper intensity in your life.

Who knows? You might even start looking differently, suspiciously, at your total mental and emotional environment, at your spouse, loved ones and your friends.

You might even start a meaningful conversation with your spouse. It can happen, it has happened.

One thing seems certain. It is worth a wholehearted try. A bit of favorable results can encourage you to stride forward.

Succeed or fail, no damage will result except, perhaps, wasting time you would probably have wasted anyway in some trifling and boring pursuit. You can always flee back to your former brainwashed cocoon with open arms, closed eyes and frozen mind. If you need help in your flight home to the fold, there are plenty of persons out their eager to reconstruct you in your former dull format for their own sake. It will always make pleasant small talk in your, or their, old age.

Selecting Different Ways of Looking at Things

Which word best describes your general attitude towards life, your society and its members? Check at least two from the following list. Are you a:

❐ Bully
❐ Conformist/Status Quoer
❐ Follower or Leader
❐ Opportunist
❐ Patriot
❐ Recluse
❐ Soft-spoken and shy
❐ Concerned Citizen tackling issues—domestic, national, world

❐ Bystander/Onlooker
❐ Critic
❐ Humorist
❐ Opinionated
❐ Perpetual loser
❐ Reformer
❐ Underdog

Add your own particular outlook:

Now choose another two of your personal characteristics from the following list. Are you:

☐ Biased (come clean, admit it, if only to yourself)

☐ Compromiser

☐ Fair

☐ Objective

☐ Subjective

☐ Optimistic

☐ Pessimistic

☐ Paradoxical

☐ Philosophical

☐ Realistic

☐ Sarcastic, sardoni, satirical, cynical

☐ Skeptical and/or a "believer"

☐ Solemn

Now, with these four descriptive phrases, start playing games with yourself by changing your personality. Your friends and relations need not know of your change. You need not change your personality in your dealings with them. Perhaps later you might really change your personality. But not now.

If you are a reformer, deliberately adopt the mental approach of, let us say, a Status Quo-er.

If you are generally optimistic, try looking at society and the world from a pessimistic viewpoint. This should not be too hard. Doesn't every (well, almost every) thinking person believe that the world has been going to the dogs since dogs domesticated mankind? Any grandparent (whose lifestyle today equals that of most noblemen a few hundred years ago) will swear to this.

Are you too solemn? Try tickling yourself into a riotous sense of humor.

If you are a bigot (some of my most interesting, myopic friends and all of my enemies suffer from this disease) try to think briefly like a liberal. And if you are already are a liberal, why not become a bigot by dripping a bit of virulent pus into your brain? After all, hate makes the world spin around just as much as love does.

If you are a leftist, try to don the cloak of a rightist.

Do you exploit your employees? Try to see things their way. But don't go overboard unless you want your wife to take in other people's washing.

Cross-fertilize between what you think you are and what you would like to be—or hate to be—between what you really are what you would like to be. This exercise should help shake you out of your mental gulag.

Changing the Themes

Changing your way of looking at issues is the next step to gain a different perspective. Start dealing with themes you have zealously avoided in the past, or those upon which you have no fixed opinion. Ignore all other made-to-wear opinions and create your own. Do a bit of self brainwashing.

Such issues might be:

- Killing all seriously defective children at birth
- Castrating all serious sexual perverts
- Exiling all criminals to an Alaskan gulag.

- Selling poisoned hard drugs, sporadically, on the street to re
  duce the number of drug addicts

Add your pet peeve that is unacceptable to society:

"Wit is the sudden marriage of ideas which before their union were not perceived to have any relation."

Mark Twain

Semi-mechanical Creative Methods

This mechanical method (also useful in solving other bedeviling problems) consists of:

Selecting and finding the relationship between two concepts. These concepts can be anything: words, processes, thoughts, conditions, situations, facts, trends, things, ideas, ideologies, causes, and so on. Anything goes.

Jettison All Assumptions

But first, we must realize that many concepts are generally loaded with deeply rooted misleading "assumptions." We must try to pinpoint and eliminate these so we can start afresh. Then we must test the new reality against common sense.

For example, it is an universally accepted "truth" that prostitution is the oldest profession. Everybody agrees with an all-knowing smirk but rarely has anyone ever dissected this truth.

Even a little thought will engender grave doubts.

Prostitution could only be defined after "morality" descended from heaven to both hound and comfort us real or pseudo sinners.

Thus, priests had to predate whores. Only a professional reformer, deeply imbued with a sense of morality, could define and stigmatize prostitution. (Or alternatively to exploit the ladies of the night to the glory of their God, that is to say, for the pleasure of his self-designated representative on earth.)

So, we can say without fear of contradiction: "The self-appointed professional, priestly representatives of God, predated the oldest profession because they received heavenly inspired messages to define prostitution. (Hmmm? Maybe the old saying is correct. Don't many so-called men of God prostitute themselves?)

Let us take another assumption, namely that Western women are responsible for the success of the Women's Liberation Movement. But this Movement would have stagnated into an entertaining life-long soap opera of small talk and little action (despite an occasional vociferous vocal feminine firebrand) with little practical results without the wholehearted support of many men.

For this Movement, despite its one-sided pro-feline (oops, sorry, I meant feminine) and misleading name, had a sneaky masculine objective: to liberate many deserving and suffering husbands and live-in boyfriends.

That men fueled this movement seems preposterous until we realize that American black slaves rode piggyback to freedom on the backs of white reformers who died to free Blacks from slavery—to leave them free to wallow in prejudice, humiliation and economic disadvantage.

To sum up: question every assumption. Every prevailing belief straight-jackets our range of thinking into preset and preformulated channels. The "other guy" decides and limits the field of battle (and all too often the timing.)

Another illuminating example of restricting our range of thinking is the timeless question:

Did God, as claimed by the Religionists, create life on earth, or did it gradually emerge from disgusting and revolting slime as claimed by the Evolutionists?

The field of battle is thus "God or Evolution." This, called "black or white" thinking, limits us to two possibilities.

Why not dredge up a third or even a fourth hypothesis?

Why not even a partnership between the Religionists and the Evolutionists?

Defining Our Concepts

Now, let us move on to another vital factor, namely, to examine and define any two concepts from as many as possible angles until you understand them better, until they fit into the general scheme of things.

The two concepts we have chosen to illustrate our method are "politics" and "doctorates."

One good way is to play the ancient game of 20 questions. Let us take the word "politics."

Some questions:

- Are politics really needed in our world?
- What exactly do politicians do?
- Must politicians always compromise?
- Do politicians need the backing of a party?
- What type of a person is attracted to politics?
- How can we attract better people to politics?
- Do the best people avoid politics like the plague?
- Politics corrupt but does politics corrupt absolutely?

Keep on asking questions and write them down.

Now, do the same with "doctorates."

The next step is to compose an aphorism by linking "politics" and "doctorates" by using one or more of the following methods:

Free Association, Brainstorming, Looping, Clustering, and Networking.

These five methods are essentially variations of the same basic principle of liberating the mind from its shackles of homegrown stultifying logic, brainwashing education and worn out tradition.

Let us define each one separately:

Free Association consists of uttering the first thought that pops into your mind following stimulation by another word, phrase, or idea.

Brain Storming expands Free Association by utilizing the interplay of ideas from several participants.

Looping is using Free Association to write anything that flows from your fingertips, both good ideas and bad nonsense.

Clustering consists of forming a chain of free associations; each link in this chain can start a new chain, and so on.

Networking (known as "surfing" on the Internet) involves seeking information from a string of outside sources. Mr. "A" refers you to Mrs. "B" who sends you to Professor "C" and so on.

Hopefully, by now the two concepts, "politics" and "doctorates", seem a bit closer to an aphorism, although to most of us they still seem worlds apart. But remember: everything in this world is related in some form or manner.

(Some even claim that man evolved from some relative of the ape family. Of course, this is sheer nonsense. Anyone studying the mess the world is in will certainly agree that the exact opposite is true, namely, that the apes are descended from man.)

Now, let us try to awaken creative abilities by forging a connection between these two unrelated concepts by finding linking "free association" factors.

This mutual relationship concept can be anything.

Logical Approach

Let us look for common denominators.

- How are these two words, or ideas, concepts, alike?
- At what point do they meet?
- What is the possible relationship between them?
- What is the improbable relationships?

Most relationships are based on an emotion, especially such old standbys such as love, hate, revenge and pity, due process of law, time, motion, size, growth, domination, sidetracking, ostracizing, education, and so on. In short, anything. Select the most probable emotion to connect the two words:

- Love and/or hate (our eternal standbys)
- Loyalty
- Exploitation
- Conspiring
- Cursing
- Equality
- Expediency
- Capricious
- Desertion
- Formality
- Pursuit of Happiness
- Misuse •Perfection
- Remedy
- Devotion
- Betrayal
- Cooperation
- Back-stabbing
- Blessing
- Inequality
- Expendability
- Escape
- Rejection
- Excuse
- Bribery
- Health
- Healing •Safety

That are many, many more. Consult any Thesaurus.

List your own:

Here is a rather long list (it could be much, much longer) of possible question to ask yourself about the relationship between the two concepts. Several should fit your particular situation. But read them all, for they might stimulate your subconscious. Their objective is to simply shake you out of your normal method of thinking.

Recall past precedents
Look at things from all angles, superior, inferior, lateral, priority, logical, sequential, mathematical, alphabetical.
Visualize, emotionalize, dramatize, verbalize
Look for multiple causes
Look for multiple effects
Look for multiple definitions
Think about advantages and disadvantages
Are you confusing cause and effect?
Are you confusing supply and demand?
Are you confusing symptoms with causes?
Are you confusing advantages and disadvantages?
Are you confusing activity with achievement?
Are you confusing means and ends?
Are you confusing right and wrong?
Are you confusing action and reaction?
Are you confusing a generalization with a particular?
Look for checks and balances
Try both deducting and inducting
What side effects can be expected?
What ramifications?
Who profits?
Who benefits?
Who loses?
Who can get hurt?
Who pays?
What are the weak spots?
What are the strong spots?
What can go wrong?
What can backfire?
Why does or doesn't this work?

What if:
This will not happen?
This had not happened?
I didn't know that this had happened?

Ask:
What else can happen?
Why choose this and not that?
Try to cut corners, try to be more efficient.
Find short cuts in your thoughts

Ask:
Is the glass half full or half empty?
What are the alternatives?
Is this rational or irrational?
What is concealed in this concept?
What is the exception that proves the rule?
Are you putting patch on patch?
What is new, outdated, odd, curious, ridiculous strange, interesting, dynamic, silly?

Play around with the facts:
Maximize and/or minimize
Try to visualize the future. Both your personal and mankind's future.
Try to imagine things in one week, one month, one year, 10–20 years, one generation.
How can this problem be solved?
Differentiate between intentions and results
Judge by results, not intentions.
What is more enjoyable, the journey or the goal?
Adopt a devil's advocate viewpoint by seeing things through the minds of your friends, enemies, and neutrals.
How would this problem be regarded by Einstein, Freud, Lincoln, your mother and/or father and or your brother and/or sister, your best friend?
Think pro and con for them.

Box yourself into a mental corner:
Deadlines can be used, but setting a time limit may cause some persons to freeze yet inspire others to concentrate to best exploit the approaching deadline.

Since necessity is said to be the mother of invention, put yourself in a tight spot so you will have to use more energy in finding a solution.

Who was it that said, "There's nothing like a hanging to make a man concentrate"?

Illogical approach

Now, if the logical approach didn't work, let's try the illogical approach.

Above all, ban all critical judgment. Turn off that side of your brain that sits judgment on the logic of your thoughts. Lift mental limitations and ignore fixed laws. Let your imagination run amok.

The crazier and weirder the ideas, the better the final results.

Many of these wild ideas may seem outright silly, even not to the point. Don't ignore them as stupid. These weird, out-of-the-way mental joggers often are those most likely to prove effective.

View things from ridiculous, impossible situations and conditions.

Assume, conjecture, guess, hypothesize, exemplify, conceptualize, symbolize, exaggerate, fanaticize, and empathize.

Consider long shots by carefully examining your gut feelings, hunches, and intuition, before you reject them as nonsense.

Ask all sorts of silly, stupid, illogical questions:
Is the glass half full or half empty?
Why did the chicken cross the road?
How high is high?
How long is a piece of string?

Returning to Normalcy

Now, lets take another look at our two concepts, politics and doctorates. We've tested them against many of the brain stimulants listed above.

Free association of "politics" gave us:

Corruption bribes, deceit, lies

Compromise, wheeling and dealing

Garnering votes through speeches, TV appearances, kissing babies, licking ass

Power, leadership, covertly stabbing the opposition in the back, rising to top by forming a "faction" within the party, weakening the opposition

Election promises to improve conditions through reform programs aimed at introducing modern methods of efficiency, weeding out the dead wood, and so on.

Divide and Rule

Add your own ideas:

(Let's ignore the cynical thought that just sprang uninvited into your minds, namely, that most so-called reform programs are aimed at "reorganizing" and introducing state-of-the-art methods so "our friends and supporters" can be upgraded to better jobs and "our enemies and opposition" can be downgraded to minor posts or alternatively kicked upstairs to become titled figureheads without real power.)

"Doctorates" conjures up images of:

An academic life, thoughtful pipe smoking, pulling at one's beard, libraries, keep your paws off the coeds
Research, writing volumes about things of microscopic importance
Sabbaticals, educational junkets
Publish or Perish (largely replaced with "Find Funding and Grants or Get Out)
Committee sessions to improve teaching methods,
Research aimed at improving the world and understanding mankind, and so on.
Undermining your colleagues
Add your own ideas:

The only place where these "politics" and "doctorates" seem to meet is that both say (and maybe actually believe) that they want to improve conditions. Our "linking" word then is improvements.

What other ideas have we dredged up? "Weakening the opposition" and "divide and rule."

Thus, any improvements proposed by academics and not sanctioned by politicians weakens the latter's position vis-à-vis the voting public and the intellectuals have become the opposition.

After establishing these common links, let us consider the connection from different angles and viewpoints. There are endless possibilities.

Remember, earlier you decided to change your outlook from pessimistic to optimistic, from liberal to bigot, and so on.

Now is a good time to take another choice and look at this link or links from an angle you would not usually use.

(It might be a good idea to refresh your memory by reading again "Different Ways of Looking at Things" for the same concepts apply here.)

So take politics, doctorates, and divide and rule, and consider them from as many different angles as possible:
- Economic, financial
- Ideological, political, liberal, conservative, socialist
- Radical left, right, center, majority, minority, pluralistic
- Emotional, enthusiastic, fair friend, hostile, humorous
- Ethical, moral, immoral
- Ethnic, religious
- Childish, adolescent, youthful, elderly, old age
- Cynical
- Failure
- Surrealistic, symbolic

- Married or unmarried
- Justification
- Legal, due process of law, illegal, guilty, innocent
- Patriotic
- Realistic
- Feminist, permissive society
- Superrace
- Underdog

Hold back from voicing your thoughts to others. This is especially crucial if you are shy for you might be persuaded to take a different route. Even the brash might have their line of thought twisted by outsiders at this point. You could be thrown off the path your mind is working on.

So, scribble your thoughts in a special section in your secret journal. They won't show on your face. Nobody need know them—unless you want them to. If you decide to keep your scribblings, you can always keep them under lock and key.

If they begin to haunt you, if they dance a jingle in your mind, if they do become an obsessive refrain, try exorcising them by writing them down on a scrap of paper. Then burn this piece of paper. Do this ceremonially. In a darkened room with black candles. If this method works for millions of primitive people around the world, it may work for you. At any rate, it is worth a try. What do you have to lose?

The next crucial step:

Feed your subconscious all variations, viewpoints, ideas, of facts, about these two words, "politics" and "doctorates." Give your mind a large selection to sift through, to play around with, and to discard.

Now stop. Cold turkey.

Incubation

Deliberately switch off your conscious mind as much as you can. Let ideas, chaotic and confused as they may seem, stew, simmer and gestate and develop their own personalities. Let your subconscious begin its intricate process of crossing and recrossing wires to create that type of erratic short circuits that spawn illogical dreams—dreams that confound honest psychiatrists but are the livelihood of charlatans, witch doctors, crystal ball gazers, card readers, and astrologers. Give your subconscious a free hand to churn out a logical connection from the turbulent turmoil.

Yes, let your subconscious work; after all, you've worked all your life to stock it with layers of information which have enriched that muddle in your brain.

The subconscious mind often seems to work best when the conscious mind is busy with other things or when the conscious mind is turned off in sleep.

Suddenly, (if all goes well) your subconscious will spawn forth a sudden "revelation."

As noted, this often happens when one drifts off to sleep, during a dream, the second when one wakes up with a dream drifting away, or early the next morning. But a solution can come, any place, anytime. When it does, make sure that you are prepared to capture the wail of the new born baby on paper or on a tape.

The System in Action

We thought about these two words, "politics" and "doctorates", for a brief time in the evening, went to bed, recalled briefly all the Free Association material, fell asleep and let our subconscious go to work. In the middle of the night we awoke with the aphorism below fully formulated in our mind. We captured it before it could escape into limbo.

"Politicians invented doctorates to shunt society conscious intellectual reformers away from cleaning up dirty politics."

True, it is "heavily worded", but it can be honed and refined.

If You Fail, Start Over

What happens if you can't find a "linking word or idea"? Simply start your Free Association again, but this time by branching off from corruption (the first idea that politics produced) or from intellectuals, (the first idea that doctorates produced.)

Free Association of corruption gives us Mafia, etc. From Mafia we get "families" which gives us assembly belt murder, protection, prostitution, drugs, gang warfare.

The first word of doctorates gives us intellectuals. From this word we get thinkers, philosophers, and so on. Now, try to find a common denominator from these offshoot groups.

The same system can be used on the next word, "compromise", and so on down the list.

Some More Examples

Let's try to connect another two concepts: abortions on demand and society.

Free Associations for "abortions" can be: unwanted pregnancies, unwanted babies can become problematic children, unmarried mothers, murdering an embryo, permissive society, and so on.

For "society" we have: modern, progress, healthy children without psychological problems, common sense, burden on society, every child needs a father, abortion sanctioned if future baby is genetic defective or if mother cannot raise child properly due to her mental condition, education, or economic circumstances, and so on.

The connecting words for abortion on demand and for society are "unwanted babies become problematic children" and "burden on society."

The resulting aphorism:

"Any girl in this modern age who has an unwanted pregnancy should be forced to have an abortion since she lacks enough common sense to bring up properly a child without it becoming a burden on society."

Here is another exercise in connecting two concepts:

Erectile dysfunction (the modern term for old-fashioned impotence) and platonic love. Keep these two concepts in mind while starting the creative process flowing by examining the following words:

Erectile dysfunction gives us: Sex, pornography, platonic love, happiness, making the best of a bad lot, and so on.

Platonic love gives us: Loneliness, intellectual conversations, mind is more important than the body, and so on.

Our modest contribution: "Erectile dysfunction often gives birth to platonic love."

Or let's take two other words, champagne and sex.

A little thought will give you:

"Champagne induced laughter is the best exotic foreplay."

Come on now. You can easily do better than that:

Once you master the two word method, you can move on to working with three, or even more, words.

Let's take three words such as: diagnosis, prognosis and autopsy.

Diagnosis makes us think of: pinpointing the cause of sickness, medication, second opinion, and so on.

Prognosis reminds us of: prediction, comforting words, getting paid before the patient dies, and so on.

Adjectives for autopsy can be: discovering cause of death, wrong medical treatment, cadaver, and so on.

Why not say: "An autopsy may not always verify a correct diagnosis, but it always confirms a bad prognosis."

Let us take these three words: medical advances, overpopulation, and ecology.

It is widely assumed that overpopulation in many third world countries is caused by the lack of knowledge of birth control (or the refusal to use such means.)

Medical advances give us: saving lives, inoculations, antibiotics, and so on.

Ecology gives us: nature in balance, don't poison our rivers, preserve the rain forests, save the endangered species, and so on.

Overpopulation gives us: hunger, diseases, plagues, ignorance, and wars. All help to keep the population more or less stable.

What breaks this population balance and causes overpopulation and an ecological unbalance?

Why not medical care and health measures saves lives but lead to overpopulation, thus unsettling the human ecological balance.

The aphorism could run something like this:

"Medical science has created a looming human ecological time bomb in the third world."

But not, of course, in the West where people fornicate mainly for pleasure, not for procreation.

Let us delve into an idea that should upset your equanimity. Let us discuss good, evil and progress in their broadest sense.

Since progress destroys the harmony of the lives of solid citizens, understandably they fight to maintain the status quo. These respectable citizens view as evil those equally good citizens demanding progress that must eventually upset the status quo. Turmoil and turbulence will replace stability and contentment.

But those good people pushing for progress regard the stubborn status quoers as backward, as obstacles to a better future.

Now, which side is good and which side is evil?

Write two aphorisms. The first should depict the status quo-ers as evil; the second the exact opposite.

What emerges from this little exercise is that good and evil depend (in this case) on your built-in assumptions, not on abstract principles.

Now, watch the evolution of connecting four words: husbands, wives, careers, unhappiness.

The first attempt produced: "Few husbands are happy if their career wives outshine them."

This was refined to: "Successful career wives rarely have happy husbands."

Some time later, this phrase jumped fully formulated from my subconscious: "Behind ever successful career wife there is a jealous and envious husband."

Of course, it is a variation on the chauvinistic feminine theme: "Behind every successful man there is a woman."

Your Specific Approach

Now, try your hand at connecting any two of the words listed below.

This list is but a drop in the bucket. You can easily expand it greatly by simply leafing through any Thesaurus, by opening a dictionary one page after another at random and selecting the first noun, verb or adjective that catches your eye.

Ability Abortion Absurdity Achievement Action Adolescent Adultery Aggression Agnostic Aims Altruism Ambition Anarchy Anger Appreciation Arrogance Artificial Atheism Authority Bad luck Banality Bashfulness Beliefs Betrayal Bigotry Blackmail Blunders Boasting Boredom Bravery Bribery Causes Celibacy Chance Chaos Charlatan Cheating Childish Circus Clowns Commitment Compassion Complaints Conceit Confidence Conflicts Conformity Conquest Conscience Contempt Cooperation Courage Cowardice Crime Divorce Doctors Drugs Ecology Equality Ethical Expedient Expendable Faith Fashionable Fear Fighting Frustration God Good luck Narrow minded Promiscuity Punishment Revenge Sanity Secrets Sex Sin Slander Snobbery Stupidity Trap Vice Whoring Winning Narrow minded

Add your own suggestions:

Now try to connect any of the three words below:
Praise, flattery, revenge
Bastard, good man, trust
Devils, saints, dependability
Love, sex, commitment, trap
Punishment, education, failure
Traveling, defeat, senile judges
Traffic murders, police failure, bravado

Polishing and Condensing

Sometimes the idea of an aphorism is so startling in its clarity that it needs little or no refining; sometimes the idea comes fully formed but must be reworked, rewritten, and repolished, again and again, until its meaning is crystal clear.

Cast the basic idea in different molds until it clicks in your head.

An old journalistic trick in condensing is to remove one or more words from each sentence. This might force you to rearrange your sentence in a different pattern. After doing this rearrangement, try repeating again this "one word out" exercise.

Here is an example:

"Water which is too pure has no fish." Ts'ai Ken Tan

Striking out one word (which) from this eight word sentence gives us:

"Fish cannot live in too pure water." (Seven words left.)

Another word (live) comes out to give us "Too pure water has no fish."

Removing "too" results in: "Pure water has no fish."

Doesn't this five word sentence have just as much impact as the original eight word one?

Another example: "We never know the worth of water until the well is dry."

Why not: "We value water only after the well has run dry"?

Note that the negative expression "we never know" has been changed to a more positive one, "we value water."

Avoid the passive tense; the active tense adds clarity, brevity and vigor.

Avoid lifeless words of the "to be" and "to have" families: is, are, were, have, had, and so on.

Test not only each word by itself, but choose words that make your meaning crisp, clear and sparkling.

Don't worry if you handiwork is contradictory, if one contradicts another in an outrageous fashion. Be thankful that you have learned one of the secrets of life; life is one long contradiction.

Beware of over-polishing. The clever idea, so firm in your mind, can be whittled away to become a blurry puzzle to others. Over concentration on the beauty of words and phrases often obscures the meaning.

Be suspicious of anything that seems too good. You may be conning yourself. Check your fantasies against reality.

Rewrite the following using the "one word out" method:
"The first step to learn in surviving your children is to accept the fact that parents can do no right, children can do no wrong."

Cooling Off Period

After you have polished and honed to a fine edge your beauty, put it away for a while—at least a week, but much better for a month or two.

Then examine it with the traditional jaundiced eye of a professional writer. Ask yourself: Is it logical? Is it reasonable? How does it jibe with today's reality? Does it contain contradictions?

Does it say what you want to say?

Is it too slick?

Does it sparkle or fall flat?

Does it hook you?

Have you rewritten something you heard in the past?

How will others understand or misunderstand it? Does it still have the same charm? The same penetrating insight? Or does it appear silly and vague?

If the latter, try rewriting it. If the former, congratulate yourself.

The nicest thing about aphorisms is that if at this stage you discard one as unsatisfactory, you can always try to make it work at a later date.

You will never reach perfection no matter how hard you try. Perfection simply doesn't exist. At least not on this earth. But trying to come as close as possible to mining your own talents has its own reward.

Criticism

Show it to friends. Don't shy away from constructive criticism. Their comments can be helpful.

But don't let others discourage you. They may have ulterior reasons for either praising or discouraging you.

As noted, any halfwit, armchair intellectual can find fault in any act of genius.

As George Burns said: "It's too bad that all the people who know how to run this country are busy driving taxis and cutting hair." One might extend the list to include bartenders and columnists, but not writers of aphorisms. For the latter are constantly seeking, analyzing, examining, rejecting, and again seeking—the truth.

But be wary of showing your brain-babies to those of your acquaintances (especially relatives) who habitually belittle anything that does not enhance their glory, who feel great only when they make others feel insignificant. If you should, however, regrettably fall into the hands of such a destructive critic, play a little game.

Listen patiently until he finishes. Then look at him oddly, obviously trying to hide your pity. Then tell him you mistakenly gave him not one of your aphorisms, but one of the most famous ones in Korean or Japanese or Chinese.

Explain that some untutored minds in the West find it difficult to step outside the limited bounds of their own culture to grasp the subtleties of ancient eastern civilizations. He will wither internally.

Incidentally, either get rid of this "friend" or parody him by turning him into an aphorism.

One thing seems certain. If you are naive, and your naivete shows, you will be spotted almost immediately. They will victimize you with laughter.

Plagiarism

About this time you will develop a sickening feeling that your aphorisms are badly tainted by plagiarism, especially those that sound too clever to be homemade. This suspicion might be mild, but again it might be vigorous enough to upset you for days. Delicate souls may even want to throw up.

This sensation of plagiarism may plague you whether they leaped fully formed from an inspired mind, or whether they followed laborious work and research.

(Remember the difference between plagiarism and research: Plagiarism means stealing from one person; research means stealing from many.)

How is it possible, you ask yourself, that someone else has not stumbled onto the same idea during the centuries? Aren't you regurgitating something you have read or heard in the past, something mired in the inner recesses of your mind, something which your subconscious might have jarred loose due to looking at the world from another angle?

It might be a good idea at this point to see if you are really unconsciously plagiarizing. Compare your brain bastards with contemporary ones. If they are almost identical, don't hide your head in shame. You will be surprised how many scientific discoveries reach fruition at the same time since the conditions are ripe. If you have been copying, console yourself: the wisdom you have written has become part and parcel of your life.

Even if you are duplicating someone else, don't ask yourself why you should go to the time and trouble, and sometimes the mental agony, of formulating them? Why not read what others, wiser than you, have thought up?

A good question.

But then why play chess, cards, and baseball? Why do anything? Why have sex? Why fall in love? People have been doing this before man descended from the trees, or rose up out of the slime.

Because the joy is in the doing, in acting out and in expressing yourself.

Who was it that said: The journey is more important than the destination? (If you have a good memory, you will come up with several authors.)

Wisdom is Ageless

Well, to be perfectly honest, often your brainchild has indeed been formulated in almost the exact same words centuries ago.

For example, once thoroughly irritated by the bad manners in Israel (it could easily have been New York), I exclaimed: "It's easier to take the Jews out of the ghetto than it is to take the ghetto out of the Jews."

I was quickly informed that this anti-Semitic witticism had been formulated generations before I was born.

Don't worry too much about plagiarizing. Ideas (which are definitely limited in supply) can't be plagiarized, only their specific form. And even if you come up with an almost identical phraseology, there is little likelihood you will be sued. And if you are sued, you might become a bit poorer, but you might also become a very short-lived celebrity. So bask in your split second of fame. Even plagiarists can become heroes.

So, if your friends say that your pet creation rings a bell in their minds, they are probably right.

Believe me, the basic idea of any aphorism has been formulated already—unless you are an Einstein or a Freud, and even they built on their predecessors. If you want to be facetious, you can comment: "Another time when two great minds think alike."

Take the aphorism: "Trite is true."

Did I really write this? I doubt it myself.

But where did I read it?

I haven't the faintest idea.

Anyway, it is so trite and so true that many, many others must have thought about it, even wrote it down.

Or: "In my youth I knew all the answers; now, in my old age I don't know what questions to ask."

Is this an original idea or did some wise and ancient Greek philosopher utter it in the far distant past.

In the final analysis does it really matter?

Did I really write compose this one? I doubted it myself even as I was writing it.

If some one claims it was written by some ancient Greek philosopher, I'll agree without arguing—and without shame.

The main purpose of "wisdoms" is to imbibe a bit of wisdom, to get a better hold on life. You can accomplish this just by reflecting on this idea. Does it matter if it is yours or someone else's?

(But is "Trite is true" really true?)

As someone said, "All generalizations are untrue, including this one."

And if an aphorism evokes an uneasy *deja vu* feeling, it is probably because the basic idea, but not your particular choice of words, has been lost in antiquity. The same thought appears again and again throughout the ages with different variations. (Mankind learns slowly, oh, so slowly.) Each era rediscovers the basic idea and formulates it to fit the times.

A few thousand years ago Aristotle said: "No great genius has ever been without some madness."

An updated version is:

"Genius is more often found in a cracked pot than in a whole one."
E.B. White

On the other hand: "The concept of genius as akin to madness has been carefully fostered by the inferiority complex of the public." Ezra Pound (What else could he say? He was confined in a mental hospital from 1946 to 1958.)

Another example: "A prophet is honored everywhere except in his own country."
Free translation of Matthew 13.57.

"No man is a prophet in his own city."
Middle Ages Hebrew literature.

"An expert is an ordinary man away from home giving advice."
Oscar Wilde

Let's take one that is evidently as old as the relationship between men. It first appeared in Western civilization when Hillel the Elder was asked to explain the teachings of the Torah (that vast body of wisdom and law contained in Jewish Scriptures and other sacred literature and oral tradition) while standing on one leg.

Hillel replied: What is hateful to you, do not do to your fellow men. (Hillel the Elder continued: "All the rest is commentary.")

The first half of this saying appeared later as the Golden Rule of Christianity: "Do unto others as you would have others do unto you."

Yet, this principle evidently arose spontaneously in different religions such as the Bahai, Hindu, Zoraster, Buddhist, Muslim, and so on.

But who really knows? Perhaps religions plagiarize?

In conclusion, not all of us are plagiarists. About 0.0001 per cent have original ideas. Most of the rest of us are unconscious plagiarists; a mere handful are conscious of what they are doing.

In the latter two cases let us not criticize, but only remember if we were not always copying the wisdom of others, we would be mental toddlers.

There is Plenty New Under the Sun

"There is nothing new under the sun," 'Kohelet', Ecclesiastics said several thousand years ago. Of course, the Preacher (the name for Kohelet in English Bible translations) was speaking of human relations—of hate, love, jealousy, betrayal, war and peace, ethics, morality, honesty and integrity; those concepts that make the world spin around and around in its ongoing, present mess.

But the Preacher was wrong, for there is plenty new, at least under the scientific sun. It has been centuries since the universe spun around the earth; since mankind considered itself the center of all things; since the flat earth theory was discarded; since a handful of philosophers realized that mankind was only a highly unstable form of species infected with self-destructive impulses.

Today, we also have the atomic bomb, telephones, cellular phones, radios, cars, trains, airplanes, the Internet, the man on the moon, space stations, cloning, genetic engineering (which has only a slight resemblance to breeding animals,) and so on.

There is also plenty new in the human farce.

For example: expensive free love, human rights, divorce on demand, assembly line abortions, a vigorous drug subculture, and above all the magic belief in a system of self-regulation called democracy that allows a goodly portion of mankind to go undernourished while another goodly portion runs from diet to diet to melt away flabby fat.

Mighty Oaks

A parting word: Aphorisms are insights distilled and redistilled to their essence, their core, and then polished to brilliance. This process can be reversed.

These kernels of truth can be expanded into "Letters to the Editor." Many editors are eager for brief items to brighten up their lifeless op-ed pages made dull by jaded editorial writers. Moreover, the Internet is rife with "forums" seeking interesting contributions so they can attract readers—and advertisers.

Many aphorisms can easily grow into small or even long essays, into a short or wordy book.

If this seems an exaggeration, take the three word sentence "Love is Blind." If you write down all the thoughts this terse phrase evokes you have the basis for at least one hefty book. The perspective condensed into one brief thought constitutes an acorn from which a mighty oak can grow.

Here are a few more short phrases that warrant lengthy books. Select one which you think you can develop into a tome, into a doctorate.

No woman is allergic to diamonds
A man without a problem really has a problem
Time is money
We are all failures
Business is business
The show must go on
Curiosity killed the cat
Any man's death diminishes me
There is no such thing as a free lunch
The rich get richer and the poor have babies

So far, we have dealt with serious subjects, hopefully with a humorous touch, to cater to that handful of serious persons who really want to understand the world they inhabit. They are a small audience but a highly silent one.

But be warned:

Mass audiences don't want to be reformed or even informed. They want only to be amused and flattered. They don't want sermons and lectures.

So, don't be too preachy; don't lecture.

They want to smile, not to scow. They want their soul to be uplifted, not depressed. They want fulfillment of their hopes and unlimited happiness at someone else's expense. They want the proverbial "happy ending" of the American dream. These are serious times with frivolous people without great leaders.

So, if you can, give them a "happy ending."

It will also make you happy, if a bit cynical.

Perhaps your personal happy ending will not be in writing aphorism but in developing your skills in coining punchy and seducing one-liners so desperately needed by corporations suckering consumers into buying unneeded goods and useless services.

Politicians will seek you out if you can supply them with election phrases. Election campaign managers constantly need them.

But to succeed in fooling voters time after time, you should be a reasonable accurate facsimile of a human being with the gift to latch your campaign promises on the eternal hopes of life's failures. After all, you are trying to communicate with your fellow human beings.

Alternatively, you may greatly step up your ability to wisecrack and to spout out repartees. You may also make likeable new friends, or hateful enemies. Both are needed to make the world spin around.

Quoting them as wisecracks to your friends is a novel and interesting way of showing off in making small talk more interesting.

If this doesn't work out, why not make a hobby of collecting those wisdoms that especially appeal to you? Why not quote them, and especially their authors, now and then to show your erudition and wisdom? But limit yourself to one or two an evening with each person; otherwise you will be termed either a bore or a show-off.

Or you can paraphrase little known ones and pass them off as your own.

Whatever your decide, have fun, even if only from the sidelines while deepening your understanding of mankind's capriciousness.

My Aphorisms

What I call "cynicisms", and my non-aphoristic comments, have been culled from my scribblings: books, articles, wisecracks, or gleaned from friends and acquaintances.

Many are contradictory. The logic of one contradicts the logic of another. This should not be surprising. Being illogical seems to be very logical. Not only is life an ongoing contradiction, but any logic dealing with emotions is likely to be just as stable as the emotion which gave it birth.

If we all knew the truth, life would not be very interesting. All too often today's truth is tomorrow's hilarious joke or quiet chuckle.

In some measure, contradictions should reflect our eternal dilemma. If any of us knew the real truth, life would lose much of its tang, for then truth would stand still and there would be no progress. The cockroach clan has been marking time for millions of years.

Many have been slightly altered since they are presented out of context.

The reader is asked to weigh carefully each saying before putting a mental check mark after one or more to indicate that he finds them: silly, vulgar, banal, insipid, crude, disgusting, foolish, degenerate, inane, piercing, facetious, profound, frivolous, superficial, profane, sacrilegious, trite or whatever definition comes to mind.

If the reader has the time and energy, he/she is asked to review his initial judgment definitions. Some have a strange characteristic of changing upon reflection.

The superficial ones may appear profound—or outright stupid. Pay special attention to the silly ones. Their grain of truth might assume startling proportions.

All have one thing in common: each and every one can be improved upon. You should have little or no trouble doing so. If you feel that some of them have been plagiarized (unintentionally, let me assure you) try to trace the idea back to the original author.

Advice

The best advice I can ever give anybody is never to take advice from me.

Age
A man might be too old to bed down a woman, but he is never too old to love or to kill.

Anti-Semitism
There is no known cure for anti-Semitism for there is no known cause.

Jews need neither smoke nor fire to detect anti-Semitism; they can even detect it where it doesn't exist.

Art
Art gives you a glimpse of where you are going without telling you why.

There is more art in a French kitchen than in an American art gallery.

Ma, there is more art in your cooking than in a prestigious art gallery.

Darling wife, there is more art in your cooking than in a prestigious art gallery.

Blessings
Make your own blessings. They are the best. They last longer.

Blondes and Brunettes
Make love to blondes but marry brunettes.

Chauvinism
Female chauvinists outnumber male chauvinists two to one; they are not only more vociferous than men, but also more interested in toppling men than in helping their sisters.

More men fight for women's rights than women.

Women have sex-washed men to fight for the rights of women.

Crime and Criminals

Lie detector tests are worthless. The results depend on which liar is taking the test, which liar is giving the test and which liar is interpreting the test.

It's easy to commit the perfect crime in an imperfect world; professional criminals are more capable than professional policemen.

There is no labor exchange for an out-of-work hitman, no unemployment compensation.

The professional criminal and the professional policeman are batting the same ball back and forth over the same net. It's easy to change sides. After all, a cop is only a crook gone wrong, an innocent who chose the wrong profession after being brainwashed by society.

Crime is a lonely vocation.

Crime just isn't what it used to be, and the dollars purchasing power has gone gekockin. Even a successful criminal can hardly make ends meet.

Crime doesn't pay? Of course crime pays; it just doesn't pay well enough, and your can rarely enjoy the perks; and there is no pension.

Crime no longer is a profession. One must study to become even a quack doctor, but not to become a criminal, a whore or a journalist.

It is a heinous crime not to eliminate some persons; it is justifiable and civilized justice, the justice of murder.

Conscience is a crock of bullshit. I've never felt one iota of regret after killing a person. But then I've never killed anything who didn't deserve it.

Victims of crime arise; demand equality with criminals.

The primary cause of crime is the inability of the police to enforce the law; of the prosecution to think straight; of the judges to exploit the law in the name of justice, and of social workers that focus on the rehabilitation of criminals and not their victims.

Destiny
Most of us don't know where we're going until we arrive at the wrong destiny.

Diets
A beer a day,
Keeps the cardiologist away,
I always say.
I like that. It rhymes.
Garlic is the world's tastiest antibiotic.

Divorce
Every woman should get divorced at least once. The emotional and educational impact is equivalent to a year-long study trip around the world or a Ph.D. in psychology. A divorce is cheaper than either. It's also a good excuse for small talk, gossip, self-indulgence, self-pity, sexual escapades, and adolescent tantrums.

A woman who screws herself into a corner with the wrong man is pretty hesitant about trusting her own instincts again—unless she's a fool, or falls in love.

Dreams
Lovely dreams make harsh realities.

Ecology
Modern health methods have created the world's greatest ecological problem: overpopulation.

Education
Society needs more idiots; it already has too many geniuses.

Politicians invented doctorates to divert intellectuals from public life.

Universities teach men and women with golden hands to earn a living by using their leaden brains.

The best education parents can give their children is to teach them to fend for themselves in a clawing society.

Elections
As long as the system remains truly democratic, the scoundrels in power should be changed every four years; shaking up the establishment outweighs most other consideration.

Ethnic identity
"How did you know I wasn't Jewish?"
"When I ask you a question, you give me an answer, not an argument."

Fashions
Fashions come and fashions go; but the fashion to be in fashion always stays in fashion.

Fashions in sex come and go, but the verities go on forever.

People tire of their heroes. Every now and then they like to rip them to pieces in public and create new ones.

Foreplay
The best foreplay starts in the mind.

Funerals
Make every effort to avoid funerals, especially your own.

Future
Have not our sages, of blessed memory, in their infinite wisdom written: past truths are always open to interpretation; present truths are always open to argument; only future truths are true. But there are no future truths. The future always becomes the present before it is usable and it becomes the past before we think we understand it. Rarely is the truth we understand usable in the present or to plan the future.

I want all my tomorrows to start today.

Germans and Nazis
Decent Germans just couldn't stomach gassing Jew babies. They threw up. Not cricket.

Our German guilt was in losing World War II; losers are always guilty.

We Germans will again dominate, for we have felt our guilt only platonically; for us to really accept our guilt, means atoning for the past; sterilizing the present; castrating the future.

The Germans weren't any worse than the other Europeans. Nearly all Europeans hate Jews. The Germans were just more efficient and more honest than the others. They never hid their feelings like the other Europeans.

You got to admire Goebbels. The Nazi's conveyor belt death disassembly lines could have been built by any competent engineer without a conscience. But the emotional and mental engineering, the mustering of latent anti-Semitism, tricking the Jews, deceiving the good Germans, harnessing the best scientific minds to swallow scientific hogwash—that was sheer brilliance. Goebbel's place in history as the meister genius of masterminding minds is assured.

GOD

Even God needs a helping hand now and then.

God is not an exact science.

Both God and his Prophets, and even the Devil, are bound by the laws of physics.

Maybe we are really descended from apes. God was a monkey.

God is a Fuck-Up. I'll tell you why. It is written that man was created in God's image. Man is a Fuck-Up. So God is a Fuck-up. Simple logic. Only the Devil is on the ball.

If God had meant for people to kiss he wouldn't have put noses in the way.

Ja, ja, my God, your God, his god, in the end it's everybody's God and nobody's God. And does God have a God? And what God created God? That's the question.

In the end we all come home to God; there's simply no other place to go.

Golden Years

The Golden Years are when your hair falls out, your teeth get yanked out, your eyes go rheumy, your dreams turn nostalgic, your hopes arthritic, and your mind asthmatic, and you begin to tell yourself you're just as old as you feel.

Good and Evil

One man's good is another man's evil; one's heaven is another man's hell.

Government

The Government giveth and the Government taketh away.

Politicians, like newspapermen, have short memories. But newspapermen have their archives; politicians have their opponents to refresh their memories.

Greetings

All the best, but remember the worst is yet to come.

Characters, characters, never real people.

How am I? I'm living but this too will pass.

Why do Israelis Say "Shalom" when they meet and when they part? Because they don't know if they're coming or going.

Happiness

Happiness is a full-time hobby—almost a second profession.

Some people can't be happy unless they're miserable. Then they know things can only get better. Happiness is fleeting and unstable; misery is solid and dependable. It is much easier to find ways to make yourself miserable than it is to create happiness.

Second best happiness can be delicious, so mellow, when you're mature. Sometimes late love is lasting love. It's like an Indian summer, like old wine. To be sipped gently.

Love may strike quickly, like lightning, but happiness demands long hours of hard work. Happiness doesn't drop like the gentle rain from heaven.

Hebrew and Culture

The Israelis consider themselves a mosaic culture composed of many ethnic groups bound together by a weak religious/heritage glue and by a stronger outer pressure of persecution.

The Hebrew language is the prime passport to integration and acceptance in Israel. Among the secular, fluency in Hebrew and a knowledge of folklore have replaced Judaism as a religion and a culture.

Holocaust

Few human minds can hold the image of a loving, gracious God and an abominable, iniquitous Holocaust at the same time.

Jews today smell existing dangers. Another Holocaust will never catch them again with their pants down and their circumcisions hanging out.

The apathy of believing and practicing Christianity to the Holocaust converted Pope John Paul II from a semi-divine recluse receiving in dignified audience the devout into a hustling, huckstering salesman trying to shore up a faltering religion with his own sincerity.

The Jews can best prevent the Nazis from whitewashing Holocaust history out of existence by stressing the murders of the Goyim. Names. Dates. Figures. Camps. The families of the cremated Goyim can best convince other Goyim of the Holocaust of the Jews.

Home
Every man needs a hole he can call his home.

Honor
The list of honored professions without honor is endless. By definition you can only have honor among honorable people, and there are so few honorable people in this world. Honorable people make a piss-poor living. It takes money to raise a family, to enjoy life.

Husbands and Wives
Never let a wife get on top of you; never let her get the upper hand.

Never be too good to a wife; she might deserve it, but she doesn't expect it—it upsets the apple cart in her mind.

Idealism and Ideologies
Ideologies are like delicate hothouse flowers; they wilt quickly under the harsh sun of reality, or turn into man-eating sharks.

"Isms" have replaced religion as our guiding light.

Trust a scoundrel before an idealist; the first only pickpockets your brain, while the second blinds you with his castles in Spain.

Ingathering of the Exiles
Many Israelis yearn for the Diaspora where the Goyim kept them on their mental toes.

I may be of the Chosen People, but it is not of my choosing.

For some Jews the Israeli Homeland is not the fulfillment of their destiny, but an escape from the fulfillment of their destiny in the Diaspora.

Jewish Mystique, The
Whenever you find a brilliant Jew, look for a heavy dose of Goyish genes.

Jews are not smarter than Goyim: they just seem smarter since they are more conceited than Goyim.

What Nobel Prize Laureate looked Jewish? Practiced orthodox Judaism?

Some of my best Jewish friends are Goyim.

Jews and Christians
Christianity without Jew-baiting is unchristian.

Nobody has ever gone wrong baiting Jews.

Christianity prefers Israel as a fish bone in Moslem throats to a nail in the Christian cross.

Do not fear being called a Dirty Jew by a Mangy Goy. Both of you might be right.

Better to crucify Jews in the name of Christ, then to be a Jew crucified in the name of Christ.

Now Christ, there was a Jew Boy who really made good. But only among the Goyim, for no Jew can put another Jew before himself.

Jew are a double-edged symbiotic catalyst with the Goyim; a catalyst which brings out the best and worst in both of them.

The Jews are a barometer of the state of mentality of the Gentiles; a nation which destroys its Jews destroys its own soul.

If you eliminate Christ from the formula, the major difference between Jews and Christians is that when something evil happens, the Jews blame themselves and the Christians blame the Jews.

He was educated by defrocked Christian clergymen addicted to some kind of nutty idea that humanity took precedence over Christianity.

Christ was a circumcised Jew; the Christians can never forgive the Jews for this.

Jews and Judaism
Jews need Jews to be clever, but Jews need Goyim to be brilliant.

All Jews have had unhappy childhoods.

Jews never expect happy endings; for a Jew a happy ending is a chance to start anew.

The Jews gave the world three things: the Bible, beer and a blistering headache.

Jews aren't smarter than anyone else; those who survive at survival levels just seem smarter.

Judaism is too good for the Jews.

Germany's intellectual growth and progress has always been in direct proportion to its ability replace Christianity with overt or covert Darwinism. Christianity is a road block to progress. Thus, Hitler's main objective was to undermine Christianity, that badly cooked and morally feeble offspring of Judaism which preaches, and sometimes even halfheartedly practices, Christ's anti-progress message. Christianity had to go. To destroy Christianity, Hitler had to sever its Judaic umbilical cord. Christianity needs Judaism to survive. Can one imagine a Judenrein Christian world? They are mutually sustaining, drawing their survival strength from each other.

Journalism
Veteran Journalist: I don't believe anything I read and only half of what write.

As a journalist I wrote lies as the truth; as a novelist I write the truth as lies.

Journalists are only inaccurate reflections of the news and most news is bad.

Journalism is only an attempt to turn gossip into a pseudo-science.

Justice
Life imitates art and justice apes the media.

Killing and Killers
A killer is not a murderer. And between killings he's so kind, so relaxed, so loving and lovable.

Don't sleep with a gun under your pillow. Put it down by your balls. A man always knows where his balls are but he often forgets where his head is.

Law and Lawyers
 Some Brits pronounce players as pliers and lawyers as liars.

Who said the law was fair? The law is only as fair as judges, and judges are both lawyers and human.

The law is an ass, but lawyers are anything but assholes; they make a splendid living by quoting dead precedents to pervert present justice before legal-minded, hobbled judges.

If he had studied law and not become a criminal, he would be such an honest lawyer that they would make him a judge.

Learning
The dumb learn from bitter experience; the wise from the experience of the dumb.

Logic
Emotions have a logic all their own.

Only logic outside the human experience is not contradictory.

Love
Love is only a phantom of the mind; I don't believe in ghosts.

Love is hell when you have to play games with your loved one.

Love has initiated more misery in human relations than hatred.

Trust in love but check out your love object first.

You can't analyze love.

A woman in love loses all sense of judgment; a man in love loses all sense of proportion.

Love went out when the Pill came in.

Love is love and sex is sex and sometimes the twain do meet—when both partners are young and naive.

Where is it written that love is sane? Love and sanity are poor bed fellows.

Love defies the laws of Logic.

Love has a logic all its own.

From all my loves I have learned to love better.

Love will come with the loving.

Unrequited love is the great educator; it is also such joyous sorrow.

Manners
Abandon all hope of good manners when you enter Israel.

Israelis talk without breathing and hear without listening.

Marriage

At best, love and marriage are a game of Russian Roulette.

Some married couples actually become good friends. I've read about such cases.

It's a God given right of every wife to quarrel with her husband; after all, what is marriage all about?

I'll get married in a church but divorced in a court.

Sex is a necessity; marriage is a miscarriage of happiness.

Marriage is a Greek tragedy in modern dress.

A happy marriage is an adolescent dream. Nobody is happily married. But some couples say they are to make their friends jealous.

Being friendly with a girl of marriageable age is a miracle; sex gets in the way.

A man should choose a wife with the same care he chooses a car.

Love is a poor foundation for a rich marriage.

Middle aged divorcees are more layable than marriageable.

The most important decision a couple every takes—marriage—is based on a hormonal imbalance.

Men

A man can never understand three things: God, War and Women.

Man does not live by plain, wholesome, healthy food alone.

Men's brains are in their balls.

Man was not meant to live alone.

Men and Women

A man disappointed in love with one woman generalizes about all women.

When it comes to women, I'm like a one-man dog.

People get very close to each other in bed.

Men who lose control over their womenfolk lose control over their manhood.

Missionaries

Christian missionaries need to convert others to buttress their own belief in the Divine Trinity.

Money and Morality

Paper money is like a paper God; it works sometimes if you believe in Him always.

Money, like a woman hunting for her true husband-mate, has a morality all its own.

Neurotics

Each neurotic woman is neurotic in her own special way.

Neurotic women may be terribly interesting but they are still neurotic; a man can't build a solid future on a slippery neurosis.

Never underestimate the wiles of a neurotic woman. Never.

A neurosis can be a stabilizing factor in many a neurotic's life.

Places

No one ever died of boredom in Israel; no one ever will.

I like Acre. It's so romantic. Its like a Greek Island without Greeks.

Tel Aviv is a jittery city with a nervous twitch.

Israel has a baggy culture.

Switzerland? Huh. I tried it for three months. Almost died of boredom. Switzerland is where the half-dead go to half-live.

Problems

The human mind constantly searches for problems to solve; if it doesn't find any, it creates them.

Prostitution

Few women can be first class whores. Prostitution is an art. A first class whore has to understand music, literature, art, wines, cheeses, cooking, psychology, and above all masculine vanity. She has to sight-read each client, to sense how to conduct that sexual orchestra called a man on top of her, to lead up to a splendid, euphoric crescendo. Many whores are called but few are chosen. Most women know they can't even be third-class successful whores. That's why they get married.

Psychiatry and Shrinks

There are no happy shrinks. All shrinks need shrinks themselves. They became shrinks so they could go to conventions and not feel so lonely.

How do I know what I believe until I've been psychoanalyzed?

Rehabilitation

Instead of taxing the victims of crime to rehabilitate the criminals, we should tax the criminals to rehabilitate their victims.

Religion

A thoughtful person should change his/her religion every ten years or so. There are so many decent religions around that every person should experience a few.

Western religions no longer exist as a matter of belief but as an excuse for an argument.

All three monotheistic religions are basically the same: they contradict the laws of logic. All three juggle a complicated toy they don't understand called God. All three are philosophical excuses to love yourself and yours and hate all others and theirs while preaching the love of all mankind. All three practice the same thing: how to be a vegetarian with your friends, but a cannibal with your enemies. With your friends you break bread, with your enemies you break heads.

Rules of the Game

You had to play the game according to their rules, or they wouldn't let you play; if you played and won, they changed the rules.

Sabras

Both the cactus pear with its nasty thorns and native-born Israelis with their nasty manners are called sabras; it is a moot question which was named after which.

The sabras have been cruelly strangled to mental mediocrity.

All Sabra women have cold feet at night.

What genius has the Zionist State produced?

Sadism

A bit of sadism rarely hurts anybody; sometimes it's even healthy.

Science and Scientists

Science is a religion without a morality; scientists are true believers without a conscience.

Science is the art of reducing the beauties and mysteries of life and love to dull, uninspiring formulas.

Sex

Sex dilutes love.

Sex is a necessity; love is a luxury.

Always make love to Mozart but fuck to Beethoven. The first understood mankind's tender dreams; the latter understood a crescendo.

Sex is for connoisseurs; marriage is for the suicidal.

There are several stages in a man's sex life. In the first stage he screws because he is an animal driven by his instincts, needs, curiosity; in the second stage, he screws for his pleasure and hopefully for hers; in the third stage he screws for results in a baby carriage; in the fourth stage he screws out of habit and a sense of duty; and in the fifth and final stage he screws out of a sense of pity for his wife. A decent man doing his duty with an aging wife can face agony.

After all is said and done, man is a sex-driven animal.

Sex is an emotion-cleansing enema.

Sex is to the mind what an enema is to constipation.

Man does not live by sex alone; woman does not live by love alone.

Success

We are all failures.

Taxes

Paying honest taxes is not so certain in the Middle East; only tax collectors are.

Paying income taxes has a morality all its own in the Middle East.

Time and Eternity

The dead can't tell time.

Top

It's not lonely at the top for those who belong at the top.

Those at the top are always a bit paranoid. It goes with the territory.

Most bosses have an open door but a closed mind policy.

Traffic

If the Arabs ever want to wipe out the Israelis, they'll buy each and every Israeli a car and a bottle of Scotch. Much cheaper than planes, tanks, missiles, cannons and guns.

It is the democratic right of every driver to kill himself in a traffic accident.

Abroad, you are doubly cautious before you break the traffic laws once; in Israel, you are doubly cautious before you obey the law once. Obeying traffic laws gives you a dangerous sense of security. You think the other driver is also obeying the law.

You may only die once, but you can live in a wheelchair forever.

Truth

We two will make our own truth.

If I'm truly convinced it is the truth, it is the truth as far as I'm concerned.

We live in a changing world where new eternal truths are constantly playing musical chairs with old eternal truths.

Truth is surviving, for what survives is the truth.

Dishonest flattery is the best as long as it's convincing.

War

Bloody wars should turn thinking men into fighting pacifists.

War is the cruelest art; the loser loses everything, and the winner only wins another chance to lose.

Ridicule is the cruelest weapon.

People who fight fair don't need to fight at all. They can play golf, drink gin, cheat on their wives, and talk things over.

Men who fight together as brothers in war can live together as brothers in peace; men who die together as brothers in battle should be buried side by side as brothers in death.

It's difficult to become friends on the battle field with a comrade-in-arms who will surely have his head blown off in a day or two.

Wisdom

Wisdom is like a girl's first period and a boy's first wet dream. Both develop as a function of age.

When I was young and dumb enough to think I was smart, I thought I knew all the answers; now that I am old and smart enough to know that I am dumb, I don't know what questions to ask.

Women and Wives

Women in love. Huh. Nobody understands them because they don't understand themselves.

A woman without a man is like a homeless homing pigeon.

Women spend more time, effort and thought shopping for clothes than they do for a husband.

Women who burn like diamonds in the light are as cold as diamonds in the night

There are three things most women are ready to die for: their sexual attractiveness, their children, and sometimes their husbands.

Plenty of wives should have the shit knocked out of them; and twice as many husbands.

Friendship between women is a fuck-all when a woman's future depends on hooking her salvation. Good men are a rare commodity. Once you get one in bed, half the battle is won.

Any woman is a good cook when her man is hungry.

You can't learn about women from books; you can't even learn about women from women.

The Women's Liberation Movement has freed more deserving husbands than deserving wives.

Women fall into two main categories; the fertile who demand the right of unlimited abortions; and the infertile who pray for a medical miracle so they can conceive.

You can teach a woman to fuck better, but you can't teach a woman to play first class chess.

A woman is not a woman unless her man loves her and a man is not a man unless he makes love to his woman.

Zionism

Diaspora Zionism has been bankrupt for decades, except as a slogan, a social hobby and an expatiation.

The Middle East without Zionism will be a desert without an oasis.

Zionism has only given the world a headache.

Zionism can be more dangerous than Judaism. Judaism is mired in worshipping the past; Zionism in bulldozing a stormy future.

Zionism is normalcy; normalcy is Judaism gone to seed; normalcy is the opiate of Judaism.

Schnorring corrupts and absolute schnorring corrupts absolutely.

Annex 1

Aphorisms, and their variations, many of which are not true aphorisms in content and form, go by many names:

Adage, Apothegm, Axiom, Banality, Bon Mot, Bottom Line, Bromide, Byword, Cliche, Catchword, Conceit, Cynicism, Dictum, Epigram, Epithet, Eternal Verities, Gibe, Glib Phrase, Graffiti, Hackneyed Phrase, Maxim, Moral, Mot, Motto, Observation, One Liner, Persiflage, Platitude, Postulate, Precept, Principle, Proposition, Proverb, Punch Line, Quip, Quotable Quote, Quotation, Repartee, Repose, Retort, Saw, Saying, Scintillation, Slogan, Stereotyped Expression, Tag Line, Theorem, Trite Saying, Watchword, Wisecrack, Witticism, and so on.

notes:

Annex 2

Common sayings that form part of our culture:
A penny saved is a penny earned.
Better late than never.
Better safe than sorry.
Children should be seen and not heard.
Don't bite the hand that feeds you.
Don't put off until tomorrow what you can do today.
If you at first don't succeed; try, try again.
It's always darkest before dawn.
Laugh and all the world laughs with you, cry and you cry alone.
Look before you leap.
Never underestimate the power of a woman.
No news is good news.
Strike while the iron is hot.
The devil finds work for idle hands.
Two's company, three's a crowd.
Waste not, want not.
You can lead a horse to water but you can't make him drink.
You can't teach an old dog new tricks.
Pride goeth before a fall.
Silence is golden.
It never rains but it pours
A bird in the hand is worth two in the bush.
Practice makes perfect.
The road to hell is paved with good intentions.
You can't have your cake and eat it to.
Seeing believes.
There are no free lunches.

notes:

notes:

(